100

THINGS TO DO IN

FORT WORTH

BEFORE YOU

DIE

Cheers to making memori
and checking
the lis
♡. Celeste
Blak

Photo credit: Visit Fort Worth

100 THINGS TO DO IN FORT WORTH BEFORE YOU DIE

• •

CELESTINA BLOK

Reedy Press
PO Box 5131
St. Louis, MO 63139, USA
www.reedypress.com

Library of Congress Control Number: 2022936995

ISBN: 9781681063850

Design by Jill Halpin

Printed in the United States of America
22 23 24 25 26   5 4 3 2 1

DEDICATION

For those who keep Fort Worth feeling like
"the biggest little small town in Texas."

Photo credit: Greg TeGantvoort

CONTENTS

Music and Entertainment

Outdoors and Recreation

Culture and History

PREFACE

Welcome to one of the friendliest cities you'll ever visit, where folks still share a firm handshake and opening the door for others is not a lost art.

There's something catchy about "Cowtown" that draws folks in, be it intrigue with the city's Western heritage (yes, there are real longhorns that walk the streets, and rodeos happen year-round here) or the easy access to a booming, world-class arts and culture scene. Not to mention the inviting neighborhoods in the middle of it all and the philanthropic spirit of our community leaders.

Fort Worth is now one of the fastest growing cities in America. It's quickly emerging from the shadows of flashier Texas cities down the highway as a destination worth a stay—or perhaps even a full-on move, as witnessed by constant new development.

I think people are enamored with Fort Worth for being so surprisingly laid back, especially for a city of its size, now quickly approaching one million residents. Visitors are often astonished at the unpretentious nature of the locals. I've heard on multiple occasions from big-city out-of-towners, "I can't believe how polite everyone is."

Yes, Fort Worth is friendly, and also full of traditions. From visiting Esperanza's for a Mexican breakfast dish after church on

Sunday to loading up the cousins for the Parade of Lights during the Christmas season, I grew up with many, and a lot of them are listed here.

For visitors, the items in *100 Things to Do in Fort Worth Before You Die* will give you a true taste of what makes Fort Worth so distinctive and almost delightfully stuck in a bygone era. From taking Sunday two-step lessons to sipping the best iced tea you'll ever taste, these items showcase iconic "musts" along with newer to-do's even longtime locals are still checking off their lists.

For locals, please note that a lot of the "things" (listed in no particular order) are activities that have been around for decades, some of which may have gotten lost in the limelight of what's glitzy and newer (although there's some of that, too). By no means is everything worth doing in Fort Worth before you die included in this list. It was a challenge to narrow down items while including a wide variety of options both tenured and new. I hope this book reminds you of how authentically adorable Fort Worth is and has been for a very long time. I am truly proud to have written it.

ACKNOWLEDGMENTS

A huge "thank you" to Reedy Press, for finding me, calling me, and asking about my interest in writing this book. What a pleasant group of individuals who are extremely organized and professional, especially Amanda Doyle, who talked me through the process with enthusiasm and grace.

Thank you to my friends and colleagues who contributed so many thoughtful ideas about our beloved hometown. While Fort Worth is rapidly growing and friends often ask me about the latest and greatest, I hope this book reminds them of a few time-honored "musts" they may have forgotten.

A big thanks to the local public relations professionals, marketing folks, general managers, and owners representing so many places included in this book for providing such helpful and speedy responses to my many questions—especially during the final days of writing.

Thank you to my parents, both Fort Worth natives, for not only sharing great insights but also helping to entertain my four-year-old son Bo during my crunch-time writing hours.

Speaking of Bo, I'm sorry that I did not get to include your suggestions of fishing at Cabela's, eating at Babe's Chicken Dinner House, and playing games at Chuck E. Cheese—although all great ideas, young son.

Thank you to Josh, for always supporting my busy endeavors. From throwing wine tasting parties to writing books, my project list is wide-ranging, and you've never discouraged me once.

• •

Photo credit: John Wayne Enterprises

Photo credit: Hookers Grill

FOOD AND DRINK

1

WAIT IN LINE
AT JOE T.'S WITH A MARGARITA

In fact, make it a pitcher—you might be here a while. A rite of passage for every Fort Worthian, sipping a lime margarita from a salted logo cup while in line outside the landmark Mexican restaurant, could be considered a pastime. Some patrons plan on it. Visit the outdoor bar just past the patio entrance (bring cash) and your party back in line will be delighted upon your return. Joe T. Garcia's originated as a small barbecue restaurant in 1935 with just enough space to seat 16. Now there's capacity for more than 1,000, and folks visit in droves daily for a coveted spot on the floral-covered patio that sits on two acres. Once inside, note that there are only two choices for dinner here: fajitas or enchiladas. With pre-dinner cocktail hour complete, prepare to sit back and indulge.

2201 N Commerce St., 817-626-4356
www.joetgarcias.com

TIP

Joe T. Garcia's is cash only, but there's an ATM on-site. Visit during the week for a chance at a shorter line. Interior seating is fun, too, especially on a chilly day.

OTHER TIME-HONORED TEX-MEX

Benito's
1450 W Magnolia Ave., 817-332-8633
www.benitosmexican.com

Enchiladas Olé
2418 Forest Park Blvd., 817-984-1360
www.enchiladasole.com

Fiesta
3233 Hemphill St., 817-923-6941
www.facebook.com/fiestamexicanrestaurantTX

La Playa Maya
1540 N Main St., 817-624-8411
3200 Hemphill St., 817-924-0698
6209 Sunset Dr., 817-738-3329
www.laplayamaya.com

Los Asaderos
1535 N Main St., 817-626-3399
www.losasaderos.com

Los Vaqueros Stockyards
2629 N Main St., 817-624-1511
www.losvaqueros.com

Mercado Juarez
1651 E Northside Dr., 817-838-8285
www.mercadojuarez.com

The Original Mexican Eats Café
4713 Camp Bowie Blvd., 817-738-6226
1400 N Main St., 817-761-1890
www.originalmexcafe.com

2

VISIT ANGELO'S BBQ
ON ST. PATRICK'S DAY

Order a frozen schooner of light beer (just say "large, make it light," like the regulars) and a plate of pork ribs or smoked brisket and take in the scenery. At this barbecue institution, opened by Angelo George in 1958, the wood-paneled walls have many stories to tell. Patrons will find taxidermy of all sorts, from bears to largemouth bass, all proudly mounted by three generations of the George family. The business is now run by Jason George, grandson to Angelo and son of Skeet. St. Patrick's Day is the anniversary of the restaurant's opening, and each year Angelo's celebrates with green-hued beer and live music by Irish bagpipers. Or visit anytime for iconic, hickory-smoked Texas barbecue against which countless others are measured.

2533 White Settlement Rd., 817-332-0357
www.angelosbbq.com

TIP

Angelo's is a no-brainer for large parties. There is always plenty of open seating and customers order everything at the counter or bar, making a visit super convenient.

MORE SMOKIN' BARBECUE

Bailey's Barbeque
826 Taylor St., 817-335-7469

Brix Barbecue
1012 S Main St., 219-363-6210
www.brixbarbecue.com

Cousin's Bar-B-Q
5125 Bryant Irvin Rd., 817-346-3999
6262 McCart Ave., 817-346-2511
www.cousinsbbq.com

Dayne's Craft Barbecue
9840 Camp Bowie Blvd, 682-472-0181
www.daynescraftbarbecue.com

Goldee's Barbecue
4645 Dick Price Rd., 817-480-4131
www.goldeesbbq.com

Panther City BBQ
201 E Hattie St., 682-499-5618
www.panthercitybbq.com

Railhead Smokehouse
2900 Montgomery St., 817-738-9808
www.facebook.com/railhead-smokehouse

Riscky's Barbeque
2314 Azle Ave., 817-624-8662 (original location)
www.risckys.com

Sammie's BBQ
3801 E Belknap St., 817-834-1822
www.sammiesbbq.com

Smoke-A-Holics BBQ
1417 Evans Ave., 817-386-5658
www.smoke-a-holicsbbq.com

3

ORDER THE FRIED ONION BURGER

OUTSIDE AT HOOKERS GRILL

Don't let the name fool you—there is nothing scandalous about this hidden Fort Worth Stockyards burger shack. The outdoor-only eatery—where orders are placed and picked up at a window—remains mostly under-the-radar, even after an appearance in the hit TV Western series *1883*, the prequel to the blockbuster series *Yellowstone*. The movie set façade for the fictional Texas House of Liquor & Sport that went up around the exterior of the two-story seating area eventually became permanent. Here, fried onions are pressed into the thin Hereford beef patties, which almost fall apart between smashed, griddle-top-toasted buns. The ensemble comes wrapped in red-and-white checkered paper and is messy—and life changing. Order a "regular," which comes with mustard and pickles. Note that the location is open late-night on Friday and Saturday to accommodate the honky-tonk crowd after dancing.

213 W Exchange Ave., 817-773-8373
www.facebook.com/hookersgrillFTW

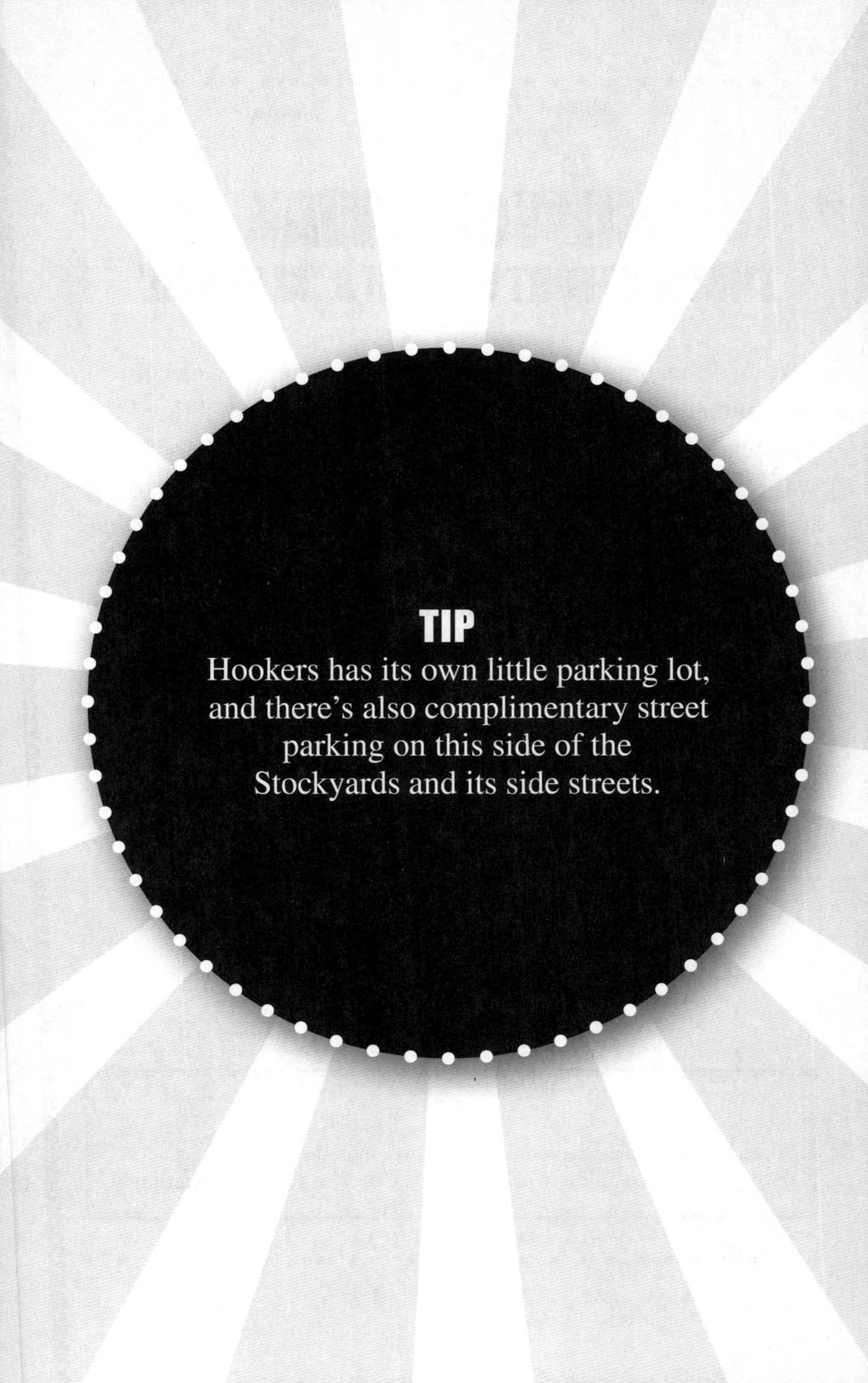

TIP

Hookers has its own little parking lot, and there's also complimentary street parking on this side of the Stockyards and its side streets.

4

SIP YOUR WAY
THROUGH FORT WORTH'S "ALE TRAIL"

Fort Worth's craft brewery scene is strong, having grown substantially since Rahr & Sons Brewing Company blazed the trail when it opened in 2004. That was back when Fort Worth was just a "Coors Light town," as founder Fritz Rahr likes to put it. Today the brewery draws thousands every week for tastings and produces more than 20,000 barrels annually. Other stops on the ale trail include Martin House Brewing Company (try the Salty Lady), Cowtown Brewing Company (get the Cold Fort Worth Beer, named for George Strait song lyrics), Panther Island Brewing (try the Allergeez American wheat ale), HopFusion Ale Works (go with the popular Feisty Blonde), and Wild Acre Brewing Company (don't miss the Texas Blonde in the pretty can with the bluebonnets).

TIP

Some breweries have taprooms open daily, and others are only open during designated tour and tasting hours. Check in advance accordingly.

Rahr & Sons Brewing Company
701 Galveston Ave., 817-810-9366
www.rahrbrewing.com

Martin House Brewing Company
220 S Sylvania Ave., 817-222-0177
www.martinhousebrewing.com

Cowtown Brewing Company
1301 E Belknap St., 817-489-5800
www.cowtownbrewco.com

Panther Island Brewing
501 N Main St., 817-882-8121
www.pantherislandbrewing.com

HopFusion Ale Works
200 E Broadway Ave., 682-841-1721
www.hopfusionaleworks.com

Wild Acre Brewing Company
1734 El Paso St., 817-882-9453
www.wildacrebrewing.com

5

SAVOR THE BACON BURNT ENDS

AT HEIM BARBECUE

Before Travis Heim started smoking pork belly cubes, no one had heard of a "bacon burnt end." Word quickly spread about the young pitmaster's sweet and tender morsels of barbecued heaven, which he launched out of a trailer in 2015. Hungry customers waited in line for hours for the hottest menu item in town, and copycat versions soon followed across the state and country. Sink your teeth into the dreamy bites at the original West Magnolia Avenue location or make the short trek to the larger River District location on White Settlement Road, where weekend live music makes for a festive, family-friendly scene. Also, visit either location early in the morning and have the burnt ends scrambled with eggs for the world's most decadent breakfast taco.

1109 W Magnolia Ave., 817-882-6970

5333 White Settlement Rd., 682-707-5772

www.heimbbq.com

INHALE THE CHIPS
AT MEXICAN INN CAFÉ

Made in-house with corn masa pressed into tortillas that are sliced into strips and then fried crisp, the addicting chips at this historic Fort Worth Tex-Mex chain are worth devouring by the bowl. They're similar to the classic Frito, although Mexican Inn's version is light, airy, and served hot. Some claim the chip originated prior to the Frito. Regardless of its history, there is no other restaurant in town that offers chips like these—the traditional, store-bought triangle version is much more prevalent. Mexican Inn dates back to 1936, when known gambler Tiffin Hall opened the first location downtown. That outlet is long gone, but there are multiple locations around town today. For extra indulgence, dip the chips in a bit of butter provided at the table. Also know that the chips are available for purchase by the bag to-go.

5716 Camp Bowie Blvd., 817-731-1126

1625 8th Ave., 817-927-8541

2700 E Lancaster Ave., 817-534-2512

612 N Henderson St., 817-336-2164

5017 S Hulen St., 817-346-7815

www.mexicaninncafe.com

7

DO THE CHICKEN DANCE
AT EDELWEISS

Schnitzel and sausage come with an accordion accompaniment at this West Fort Worth German restaurant, where, since it opened in 1967, guests have danced their way through dinner—some perhaps with a little encouragement from a beer-filled stein glass. There's live music nightly and a large wooden dance floor, so when polka superstar Helga Beckman cues for the Chicken Dance song, prepare to flap your elbows and shake your tail feathers. Some families have participated in the quirky yet amusing tradition for generations. For others, it's a one-time event. Fuel up with potato pancakes, spätzle, sauerkraut, and various wursts. Don't miss German chocolate cake or homemade apple strudel for dessert. Whether they dance or not, everyone leaves with full bellies and lasting memories.

3801 Southwest Blvd., 817-738-5934
www.edelweissgermanrestaurant.com

8

CATCH A SUNSET AND A SIP OF WHISKEY
AT WHISKEY RANCH

Fort Worth–born TX Whiskey—referred to as simply "TX" by locals—can be found in most well-stocked bars across Texas and beyond. But a short trip east of downtown is worth the drive to experience the award-winning whiskey's sprawling 112-acre home. Located on a former 18-hole golf course overlooking downtown Fort Worth, Whiskey Ranch offers the on-site TX Tavern for whiskey cocktails to order, the Ranch Store for buying bottles and gifts (don't miss the TX Whiskey coffee produced in collaboration with local Avoca Coffee Roasters), private event rooms, a small lake, and sweeping wooden porches with stone fireplaces for gathering around to see one amazing horizon sunset. Watch the event calendar for happenings like Whiskey Wednesday happy hour, cocktail classes, yoga classes, outdoor picnic days, and movie nights.

4250 Mitchell Blvd., 817-840-9140
www.frdistilling.com

9

ORDER THE FRIED COD AND A PITCHER OF BEER

AT ZEKE'S FISH & CHIPS

Look for the green and white sign with the backwards "K" just off Camp Bowie Boulevard for a trip back in time at this 50-plus-year-old institution. It's a beloved spot for fried seafood, especially the iconic Icelandic cod filets that come fried-to-order and piping hot. Neither the menu nor the atmosphere has changed much since 1971. The entry where folks line up to order at the counter is still very tight, most of the menu is still fried, and the drive-through is still busy for to-go orders, especially during Lent. Veggies here—from okra and eggplant to zucchini and mushrooms—are also all fried, steamy, and perfect for dipping in the signature scratch-made dill sauce. (Don't forget the hushpuppies and sweet corn nuggets.) Grab a seat in the checkered-floor dining room and wash it all down with a pitcher of cold beer for a perfect Friday night.

5920 Curzon Ave., 817-731-3321
www.facebook.com/zekesfishchips

10

GET RESERVATIONS
FOR A SUPPER CLUB

Once typically defined as a swanky nightclub serving dinner to well-heeled clientele while providing entertainment, supper clubs now appear in various forms. They could be one-time pop-up dinners at undisclosed locations, or in the case of chef Juan Rodriguez, a beautiful monthly gathering of 55 to 65 lucky individuals who get to partake in five courses of seasonal dishes. Rodriguez owns Magdalena's, a catering and private event venue located in a hidden nook of the North Side, where dinners usually take place outside amid his lush garden of ingredients. Menu items might range from braised elk with cherry-chipotle glaze to grilled cauliflower bisque. Seats sell out quickly for his supper club dinners (which are BYOB), so get on the email list for the best chances of getting a reservation.

502 Grand Ave., 817-740-8085
www.magdalenastx.com

11

CUT CHICKEN-FRIED STEAK WITH A FORK

AT STAR CAFÉ

Even many lifelong Fort Worthians don't know about this blink-and-you-miss-it Stockyards diner, where not much has changed since it opened in 1980. With red-checkered tablecloths, tin ceiling tiles, wooden floors, and a wonky jukebox, the Star Café provides less flash than some of the newer Stockyards establishments. Its building dates to the early 1900s, like many of the structures on West Exchange Avenue. It's situated among some of the Stockyards rowdiest bars, with Longhorns Saloon located next door, Filthy McNasty's Saloon across the street, and The Basement Bar just underneath. The motto here is, "For the best steaks in Dallas, visit Star Café in Fort Worth." It's true that, dollar-for-dollar, the steaks here are a steal. But don't miss the fork-tender chicken-fried steak. It cuts like butter and will be absolutely drowned in classic cream gravy unless you indicate otherwise. Reservations aren't needed here, and seating is often immediate for lunch and dinner.

111 W Exchange Ave., 817-624-8701
www.starcafefortworth.com

MORE GREAT PLACES FOR CHICKEN-FRIED STEAK

Drew's Place
5701 Curzon Ave., 817-735-4408
www.drewssoulfood.com

Lucile's Stateside Bistro
4700 Camp Bowie Blvd., 817-738-4761
www.lucilesstatesidebistro.com

Michaels Cuisine
3413 W 7th St., 817-877-3413
www.michaelscuisine.com

Old Neighborhood Grill
1633 Park Place Ave., 817-923-2282
www.oldneighborhoodgrill.business.site

Reata Restaurant
310 Houston St., 817-336-1009
www.reata.net

12

DRIVE THROUGH ESKIMO HUT

FOR A DAIQUIRI TO-GO

Curbside cocktails to-go aren't new to this Fort Worth booze barn, which has been serving libations through driver's-side windows for over twenty years. It's easy to miss when traveling down West Vickery Boulevard, so keep your eyes peeled for the blue Eskimo Hut sign. New Orleans–style frozen daiquiris come in countless flavor combinations, each served in a giant Styrofoam cup that is lidded and tightly sealed in plastic wrap. Fan favorite flavors include the Bob Marley, blended with strawberry, kiwi, and mango flavors, and the Purple Haze, a mix of Blue Hawaiian and Hurricane. Vodka-spiked Jell-O shots are popular, too. There are also convenience-store staples like beer, wine, snacks, and smokes—and never a need to leave the vehicle.

5518 W Vickery Blvd., 817-737-8773
www.eskimohut.com

13

BUY PAN DULCE
AT ESPERANZA'S RESTAURANT & BAKERY IN NORTH SIDE

Sunday mornings growing up in Fort Worth meant breakfast at Esperanza's after church, followed by a visit to the restaurant's attached bakery for Mexican sweet bread to-go. We weren't alone. The lines were, and still are, long at this sister restaurant to Joe T. Garcia's, located just steps away on North Main Street. Yes, there's a Park Place Avenue outlet of Esperanza's, but a visit to the North Side flagship location is a must for its energetic, almost frenzied atmosphere. Choose from dozens of breakfast pastries, but don't miss the authentic Mexican concha. Meaning "shell" in Spanish, the round bread roll with its crunchy, sugary topping in various colors is named for its seashell-like appearance. Be ready to order quickly, because folks are waiting behind you.

2122 N Main St., 817-626-5770
www.esperanzasfw.com

14

GET A GLASS OF THE ROSE ICED TEA
AT THE ROSE GARDEN TEA ROOM

Iced tea is important in these parts, and good restaurateurs know glasses should always be kept full. But there's one iced tea that's a standout in town—the thirst-quenching rose tea served at the hidden café located inside the historic Mercantile on Camp Bowie Boulevard. Navigate past the booths and antiques to find the string-lit tearoom, where ladies who lunch—and even a few fellows—visit for quiche, fruit salad with poppy seed dressing, pumpkin bread sandwiches, and glasses of iced tea. Custom blended with rose petals and vanilla and strawberry essences, the floral tea is served unsweet, although there's sugar on the table for those who wish to doctor it up. The tea is available for purchase in loose leaf form, but it's best to just let the experts prepare it and enjoy on-site (and in a to-go cup upon departure).

7200 Camp Bowie Blvd., 817-731-7673
www.the-mercantile.com/tea-room

15

DEVOUR A PLATE OF PULIDO'S PUFFY TACOS

Pulido's puffy tacos are one of the few, if not the last, left in Fort Worth. (The now-closed Caro's was popular for them for nearly 50 years on Blue Bonnet Circle.) Pulido's has been serving the crisp, puffed corn shells since 1966 and now has multiple locations, but don't miss the original on Pulido Street. That's right, the street is named for the Tex-Mex institution that remains hidden along I-30 between Montgomery Street and University Drive. The tacos, which are filled with seasoned ground beef, shredded iceberg lettuce, chopped tomatoes, and grated cheese, are easily inhaled thanks to a light-as-air, paper-thin, fried corn shell. Using both hands, lift like a tostada and expect a crumbly bite well worth the resulting mess.

2900 Pulido St., 817-732-7571

5051 Hwy. 377 S, 817-732-7871

www.pulidos.net

16

EAT ADVENTUROUSLY WITH A BOWL OF MENUDO

AT AMY'S RESTAURANT

The sign out front under the restaurant name says, "The Menudo Queen." Many agree, because Amy's fills quickly in the morning with mostly working-class men looking for a hot bowl of the traditional Mexican soup their mom or grandmother might have made during their childhood. Amy is Amy Flores, and she's built a loyal following since opening her tiny breakfast and lunch café on Fort Worth's North Side in 2007. She enthusiastically works both the kitchen and the tiny dining room to serve dishes like huevos rancheros, chilaquiles, breakfast tacos with hot, house-made flour tortillas, and the most popular menu item, menudo, a comforting soup made with beef tripe, hominy, and spicy broth served with chopped white onions and lime wedges. Her cooking is some of the most authentic in town. Don't miss the coffee. It's slightly yet deliciously spiced with a hint of cinnamon. Good thing Amy is also quick at pouring refills.

1537 N Main St., 817-841-2896
www.facebook.com/Amys-Restaurant-141470965907258

17

ORDER THE GERMAN PANCAKES
AT OL' SOUTH PANCAKE HOUSE

A sweet and citrusy taste of heaven exists in a decades-old diner on South University Drive, where the waitresses use forks to squeeze fresh lemon juice over pillowy, powdered sugar–topped pancakes dozens of times a day. These are Ol' South Pancake House's famed German pancakes, both a mouthwatering and entertaining experience thanks to the table-side preparation. What makes a German pancake different than an American pancake? Lots of eggs and no leavening agent. The result is a fluffy yet almost spongy pastry, and at this 24-hour eatery the treat takes up an entire plate. There is also a smaller version called a Dutch Baby for those with smaller appetites. For those extra hungry for a taste of Texas, ask for the off-menu Texas Chow Down, a waffle sandwich stacked with bacon, ham, hash browns, a fried egg, and cheese, dusted with powdered sugar and topped with a pat of butter.

1509 S University Dr., 817-336-0311
www.olsouthpancakehouse.com

18

LINE UP FOR A CURBSIDE MEAL

AT BONNELL'S FINE TEXAS CUISINE

Before 2020, "curbside" wasn't a term used much in the restaurant world. The pandemic changed that. But many restaurants that offered curbside pick-up only did so temporarily. Not Jon Bonnell. The beloved Fort Worth chef has made curbside cool, providing family-style meals that still generate long car lines down the Texas State Highway 183 frontage road. Bonnell announces a different comfort food favorite in the morning via social media, ranging from chicken and shrimp carbonara and beef pot pie to chicken-fried chicken with cream gravy. Each meal feeds four and comes with sides and a sweet treat for dessert. There are no reservations—simply wait in the car line and cross your fingers you arrived in time before sellout. Of course, the tenured chef and restaurateur is known for more than his curbside meals—you should also visit Bonnell's for his fancy wild game favorites, like crispy quail legs, venison carpaccio, and elk tenderloin.

4259 Bryant Irvin Rd., 817-738-5489
www.bonnellstexas.com

19

LEARN THE ORIGIN OF CALF FRIES

AT RISCKY'S STEAKHOUSE

In the early 1920s, a young Fort Worth Stockyards immigrant named Theo Yordanoff ran his namesake Theo's Café on East Exchange Avenue. When he was asked for "mountain oysters" by a hungry cowboy, Yordanoff was unfamiliar with the term. The cowboy explained the delicacy is what separates the bulls from the cows. Yordanoff quickly put bull testicles on his menu, but he renamed them "calf fries," which sounded a little more palatable. Riscky's Steakhouse now sits where Theo's once was, and calf fries are still on the menu in the home where they originated. While other restaurants in town also offer the lightly fried morsels, Riscky's is widely known for serving the best. So, if you're up for an adventurous appetizer that comes with a serving of local history, go where the dish was born.

120 E Exchange Ave., 817-624-4800
www.risckys.com/risckys-steakhouse

20

APPLAUD YOUR OWN TABLESIDE CHEF
AT JAPANESE PALACE

The theatrical show of Japanese tableside cooking, with its flips, spins, and balancing acts using spatulas much like batons, has drawn thousands to this iconic West Fort Worth destination since 1975. On the outside the restaurant looks mysterious. With Japanese-style architecture and a complete lack of windows, it remains dark and easy-to-miss during the day. But when 5 p.m. rolls around, cars fill the parking lot for a first-come, first-served table. Don't worry too much if there's a wait—the original '70s-style bar is worth hanging out in for a while. It's almost preserved in time with its sultry tones, cozy nooks, and traditional Japanese décor. Guests can choose from regular seating, teppanyaki tables for groups, and zashiki-style floor seating with cushions. Whether with a large party or for date night, dinner always comes with a show.

8445 Camp Bowie Blvd., 817-244-0144
www.japanesepalace.net

HAVE A PO' BOY
AT J&J OYSTER BAR

Make it a Jim's Po' Boy, named for the owner of this iconic seafood shack that's drawn in loyal customers for more than four decades for peel-and-eat shrimp, cold beer, and charismatic waitresses. Jim Schusler's signature sandwich comes with grilled crawfish sausage (when available) and a garnish of hot gumbo ladled right on top. The ensemble pairs perfectly with a starter of oysters on the half shell, freshly shucked within view. J&J's is cozy, with just a few tables and barstools inside amid beer signs and printed photographs from the years on the walls. There's also a breezy streetside covered patio. It's easy to stay awhile here, so seating is coveted. Don't miss the fish tacos, crab cakes, and lobster bisque (when they have it), or crawfish when in season.

612 University Dr., 817-367-9792
www.jjoysterbar.com

CHEAT ON YOUR DIET

WITH THE CINNAMON ROLLS AT GINGER BROWN'S OLD TYME RESTAURANT & BAKERY

Worth the drive down Highway 199 is a nostalgic taste of homestyle cooking, where the walls are covered with framed photos and shelves of ceramic baubles and cookie jars—perhaps a little like grandmother's house. Serving breakfast, lunch, and dinner, the restaurant has been keeping hungry diners well-fed since 1985 with its country breakfasts, chicken-fried steak, crispy catfish, and those legendary cinnamon rolls. Served all day long, the hot and buttery swirls of cinnamon dough come doused in a golden glaze of sweet icing—one that's not too thick but rather thin enough to run and almost cover the plate. No meal here is complete without one, and maybe an order of more to-go.

6312 Jacksboro Hwy., 817-237-2114
www.gingerbrowns.com

TIP

Ask for booth seating and enjoy the actual working mini-jukeboxes located at each table. Have some quarters handy.

HAVE THE FLAVOR OF THE MONTH
AT CURLY'S FROZEN CUSTARD

Whether you order from the drive-through window or sit and stay a while on the always-green, artificial turf–covered patio, visit this Camp Bowie Boulevard gem for the best frozen custard in town. Creamy and irresistible, the custard comes in just a few flavors, including chocolate, vanilla, and lemon. Then get creative with a slew of toppings or mix-ins, like fruit, shredded coconut, candies, marshmallows, pretzels, and even cheesecake bites. But don't miss the always anticipated "flavor of the month," which may range from coffee and mint chocolate chip to pumpkin and the almighty Parker County Peach, a summertime staple that arrives in July. Also in July is Curly's annual July 4th hot-dog-eating contest, which features Nathan's Famous hot dogs just like the televised national competition on Coney Island.

4017 Camp Bowie Blvd., 817-763-8700
www.curlysfrozencustard.com

ORDER A CHARCOAL-GRILLED STEAK

AT CATTLEMEN'S STEAKHOUSE

A restaurateur named Jesse Roach was instrumental in pioneering Fort Worth's steakhouse scene when he opened Cattlemen's Steakhouse in the Stockyards in 1947. Today it sits largely unchanged, with its Vegas-style signage blinking over North Main Street. Inside, steaks are prepared the way they were upon opening—over hot charcoals on a grill visible from the dining room. Yes, there are numerous fine dining establishments in town for top-notch steaks, but a trip to Cattlemen's is a trip back in time for both locals and visitors to experience a true taste of authentic Cowtown. (Wear your boots.) Steaks range from porterhouse and T-bone to ribeye and filet mignon and come with an iceberg lettuce salad, choice of potato, and house-baked rolls.

2458 N Main St., 817-624-3945
www.cattlemenssteakhouse.com

TIP

Go at lunch for great deals on great cuts. Also, don't miss the saloon bar.

OTHER SPOTS FOR GREAT STEAK

B&B Butchers & Restaurant
5212 Marathon Ave., 817-737-5212
www.bbbutchers.com/ft-worth

Bonnell's Fine Texas Cuisine (see #18)
4259 Bryant Irvin Rd., 817-738-5489
www.bonnellstexas.com

Clay Pigeon Food & Drink
2731 White Settlement Rd., 817-882-8065
www.claypigeonfd.com

H3 Ranch
109 E Exchange, 817-624-1246
www.h3ranch.com

Lonesome Dove Western Bistro
2406 N Main St., 817-740-8810
www.lonesomedovefortworth.com

25

IMBIBE BELOW STREET LEVEL

AT AN UNDERGROUND BAR

Fort Worth is home to many hidden watering holes, including a handful located below street level. Downtown there's Thompson's Bookstore, a craft cocktail bar named for a former tenant who once occupied the historic space. The main bar is located above ground, but there are two entrances to an underground speakeasy—one located behind a fake bookshelf and the other via a staircase outside. A password, which can be found on the bar's social media pages, is required for entry. A few blocks away is Scat Jazz Lounge, located in the basement of the historic Woolworth building. The swanky Art Deco–inspired scene is inspired by New York City clubs located below ground in hidden alleyways. In the Stockyards, the Basement Bar calls itself the "world's smallest honky-tonk." The dusty dive is known for its busy dance floor and cheap drink specials. Look down for the stairway entrance when strolling West Exchange Avenue.

The Basement Bar
105 W Exchange Ave., 682-841-1174
www.facebook.com/basementbartx

Scat Jazz Lounge
111 W 4th St., 817-870-9100
www.scatjazzlounge.com

Thompson's Bookstore
900 Houston St., 817-882-8003
www.thompsonsbookstore.com

TANTALIZE YOUR TASTE BUDS

WITH CHORIZO-STUFFED DATES AT GRACE

Owner and operator Adam Jones has longtime restaurant cred in Fort Worth, and his downtown gem Grace is where folks go to get fancy. While experiencing the fine dining room is a special treat, the lively bar—with its floor-to-ceiling glass windows, thick marble bar top, and street-side patio—is where one can order bacon-wrapped morsels of heaven on the menu. Chef Blaine Staniford can execute everything from squid ink pasta to scallops with caviar butter sauce with ease, but his chorizo-stuffed dates served atop a pop of orange-hued charred pepper sauce are fan favorites. They're the perfect balance of sweet, salty, savory, chewy, crispy, and plump. Wash them down with a gin martini, one of the best shaken in town. Don't forget to ask for a bleu cheese–stuffed olive as a garnish.

777 Main St., 817-877-3388
www.gracefortworth.com

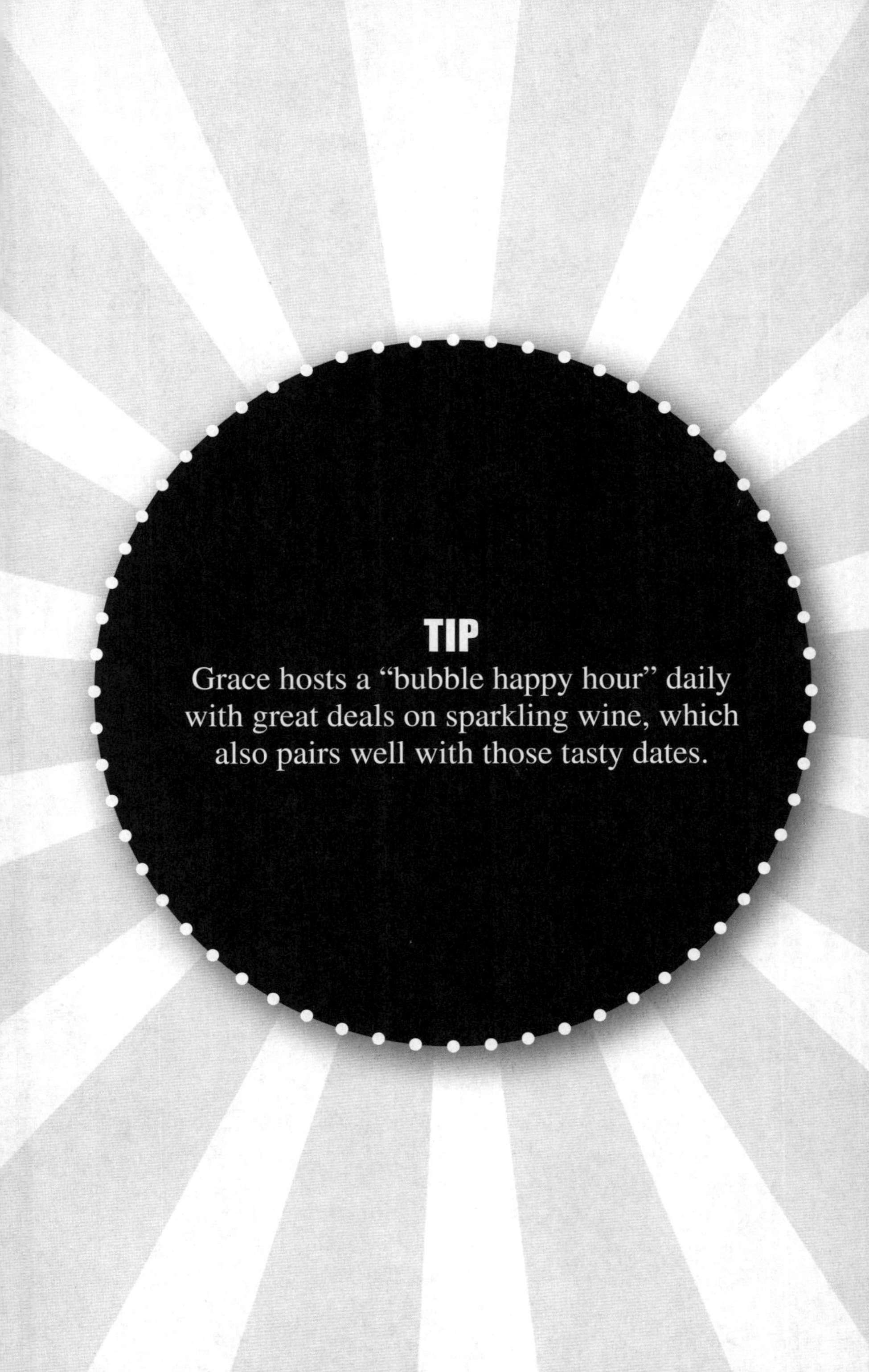

TIP

Grace hosts a "bubble happy hour" daily with great deals on sparkling wine, which also pairs well with those tasty dates.

Photo credit: Robert M. McAvoy

MUSIC AND ENTERTAINMENT

KICK OFF RODEO SEASON
AT THE FORT WORTH STOCK SHOW & RODEO'S ALL WESTERN PARADE

In Fort Worth, "rodeo" is a season, just like spring, summer, and "holiday." The season always begins with the time-honored All Western Parade, a non-motorized promenade of more than 2,000 horses along with chuck wagons and marching bands through the streets of downtown. It's touted as the "one and only" horse-powered parade. Catch the procession on the first Saturday of the rodeo; it's the perfect occasion to don your warmest western best as temperatures are usually chilly during the mid-January event. There's plenty of room to watch from the sidewalks, but a reserved seat will ensure prime views. Even better, make reservations early on one of the parade route restaurant patios and plan on brunch with a horse-and-carriage view.

Downtown Fort Worth, 817-877-2400
www.fwssr.com

28

DANCE IN YOUR SEAT
AT CASA MAÑANA'S REID CABARET THEATRE

The dome-shaped Casa Mañana theater has been around for generations, but its newer, 110-seat cabaret addition remains a bit under the radar. Opened in 2018—the same year Casa Mañana celebrated 60 years—the Reid Cabaret Theatre provides for more intimate shows that harken back to a swanky musical past. With earth-tone walls, elegant seating, and table-side cocktail service, the cabaret (named for longtime donors Molly and Rusty Reid) hosts swoon-worthy solo acts as well as lively, jump-out-of-your-chair tribute shows. Talent featured here ranges from comedians to performers who've paid homage to Bob Dylan; Whitney Houston; Crosby, Stills & Nash; and Nashville country stars, to name a few. Expect shows to last 60 to 90 minutes (with an intermission) and note that seating is cabaret-style, meaning you might sit with a new friend or two. Arrive promptly before showtime—the space is purposely cozy, and you'll stick out like a sore thumb if you're late.

3101 W Lancaster Ave., 817-332-2272
www.casamanana.org

SING ALONG TO LIVE MUSIC BELOW STREET LEVEL

AT LOVE SHACK

There's never a cover charge at this hidden Fort Worth Stockyards outdoor beer garden, which sits in a narrow, easily overlooked corridor below sidewalk level. Take the steps down to snag a wooden picnic table, or go up for balcony-level seating and a bird's-eye view of the stage as well as busy East Exchange Avenue. The acoustic sets are always sing-along worthy, with classic country and Red Dirt favorites dominating the song list. Local singer-songwriters might throw in an original here and there. The place is owned by chef and restaurant mogul Tim Love, which means the menu of burgers, hot dogs, hand-cut fries, and onion rings are of high caliber. Order the Dirty Love Burger made with freshly ground prime tenderloin and prime brisket topped with a fried quail egg.

110 E Exchange Ave., 817-740-8812
www.loveburgershackfortworth.com

30

GO BAREFOOT IN THE GRASS

AT FRIDAY ON THE GREEN

On one Friday each month from May through October, the grassy lawn located on Lipscomb Street between Magnolia Avenue and Rosedale Street comes alive with music, food, drinks, and lots of friends and families. The event is organized by Near Southside, Inc., and Near Southside Arts, who book four regional acts to take the stage in front of hundreds who come out for the fun. The pets and kids can come along, too. The event is completely free, and there's no need to bring anything besides a blanket or lawn chair, because local Near Southside restaurants and food vendors provide picnic-perfect meals available for purchase, as well as wine and beer. As the sun sets, dancing often occurs, so prepare to kick your sandals off and join in.

1201 Lipscomb St., 817-923-1649
www.nearsouthsidefw.org/friday-on-the-green.html

31

GO TO BULLS' NIGHT OUT
AT THE FORT WORTH STOCK SHOW & RODEO

A visit to the annual Fort Worth Stock Show & Rodeo, which begins in mid-January, includes multiple "musts": having a corny dog at the midway, adoring the baby farm animals in the livestock barns, taking your toddler for a pony ride, shopping from rodeo vendors, and attending at least one live rodeo performance at Dickies Arena. For the latter, two out of the two dozen or so rodeos that take place are the PRCA Bulls' Night Out, the hottest ticket of the entire three-and-a-half-week event. Attendees break out their Western best to watch 40 riders take on the rowdiest bulls. Each aim to hold on for eight seconds for a chance to be the champion and move onto the National Finals Rodeo. Go at least once to witness the fanfare or make it an annual tradition, as do many local rodeo-goers.

3400 Burnett Tandy Dr., 817-877-2400
www.fwssr.com

TIP

Tickets go on sale in the fall, so buy them early for the best seats at the best price.

Photo credit: The Fort Worth Stock Show & Rodeo

32

CHEER ON THE HOME TEAM
AT AMON G. CARTER STADIUM

Before its $164 million renovation prior to the 2012 Texas Christian University football season, Amon G. Carter Stadium—built in 1930—hadn't seen a major update since 1956, when an upper deck was added. Today the home of the Horned Frogs seats 46,000 and features multiple levels of luxury seating, clubs, and suites. With a natural grass field, raised seating bowl for enhanced field view, and upgraded concession stands, restrooms, and facilities, the stadium is one of the most comfortable in college football—from the breezy benches in the end zones to the exclusive loge boxes with personal TVs and outdoor fridges. The stadium's tailgate scene is stellar, too, so arrive early and visit Frog Alley for pre-game festivities, including the TCU Marching Band entrance led by the TCU Cheerleaders.

2850 Stadium Dr., 817-257-3764
www.gofrogs.com/sports/football

33

HAVE THE FLAMING CHEESE
AT THE FORT WORTH GREEK FESTIVAL

For one weekend in early November, thousands flock to St. Demetrios Greek Orthodox Church in North Fort Worth for its annual Greek Festival, where parishioners for decades have prepared and shared their traditional Greek cuisine with the masses. It's perhaps Fort Worth's truest taste of Greek family-style dishes, all rich with history, tradition, and flavor. Stick-to-your-ribs menu items range from leg of lamb and pastitsio (layers of pasta and meat sauces topped with creamy bechamel) to classic baklava and Greek pastries. Don't miss the saganaki—a Greek cheese that's lightly pan fried, quickly bathed in brandy, and set on fire in a flash before being served with warm pita bread. The festival runs three days, and there's no shame in making multiple trips.

2020 NW 21st St., 817-626-5578
www.fortworthgreekfestival.com

WATCH LIVE BULL RIDING

AT THE WORLD'S LARGEST HONKY-TONK

Live music, line dance lessons, and photo ops atop the taxidermy bull are a given at Billy Bob's Texas, opened in 1981 and known globally as the world's largest honky-tonk. But catching a live bull riding show here might be a lesser-known option—mostly because the arena is hidden in a back corner. (That's how big this place is.) World champion bull riders, including Tuff Hedeman and Ty Murray, have all tested their skills here, where more than 50,000 bulls have bucked over nearly four decades. Bull riding takes place every Friday and Saturday night just before Billy Bob's headlining act. It's conducted just like a professional rodeo: pro and semi-pro bull riders pay an entry fee, try to hang on for eight seconds, and take home what they win. Spectators get live rodeo action just minutes before local and national acts take the main stage.

2520 Rodeo Plaza, 817-624-7117
www.billybobstexas.com

35

BE THE FIRST IN LINE

AT DOWNTOWN COWTOWN AT THE ISIS

When you're the first to arrive at this historic North Side theater, located steps from the Fort Worth Stockyards, you get to pick which movie plays. There are more than 35 titles in rotation with several movie times each day. (Note that choices are only presented in person, not online.) Even more, all daily screenings are complimentary with the purchase of only a snack and a drink. Originally opened in 1914, the Isis Theater has endured a rough history, first being destroyed by a fire in 1935, rebuilt, then damaged again by a flood in 1942. It sat dormant, shuttered, and dilapidated for decades until it was finally purchased and restored to its original glory and reopened in 2021. With seats for 500, the theater also hosts live performances, including concerts, acoustic sets, and comedic acts. If you don't have time for a movie or a show, pop by for a classic cocktail in the swanky, 1920s-era bar.

2401 N Main St., 817-808-6390
www.downtowncowtown.com

36

SIT IN THE BACKYARD
AT HOTEL DROVER

Fort Worth hospitality was redefined with the opening of this landmark hotel in the heart of the Fort Worth Stockyards in 2021. Anchoring Mule Alley—a cobblestone street lined with century-old horse and mule barns restored into spectacular retail, bars, and restaurants—Hotel Drover offers 200 guest rooms amid an urban ranch oasis. Must-see features range from the neon cowboy light installation outside to the life-size drover sculpture made from bronze and steel in the lobby. The cornerstone of the property is the Backyard, where $4 million was invested into two acres of landscaping. Grab one of the cozy rockers or Adirondack chairs around a fire pit and listen to live acoustic Texas music with a ranch water (tequila, Topo Chico mineral water, and lime) in hand and you're doing Hotel Drover right.

200 Mule Alley Dr., 817-755-5557
www.hoteldrover.com

TIP

Book an overnight stay and you can enjoy the coveted, heated pool almost year-round.

TAKE SUNDAY DANCE LESSONS
AT THE STAGECOACH BALLROOM

Flying under the radar of flashier honky-tonks in the more touristy Fort Worth Stockyards, this country music dancehall is as authentic as they come. The Stagecoach opened in 1961, making it one of the oldest dancehalls in Texas. With its 3,500-square-foot wooden dance floor, long wooden bar, and many rows of tables of chairs, the live music venue draws a mature crowd who don their best turquoise, long skirts or sport coats, and shiniest boots. Big-name acts who've graced the stage include the Bellamy Brothers, Lorrie Morgan, Restless Heart, and many more. On Sundays the fun gets started early; doors open at 1:30 p.m., with dance lessons promptly following at 2 p.m.—no partner required, and beginners always welcome. Themes range from the familiar two-step to the classic country waltz. Stay for the house band at 3:30 p.m. to practice your new boot-scootin' moves.

2516 E Belknap St., 817-831-2261
www.stagecoachballroom.com

LISTEN TO LIVE MUSIC

ON THE CENTRAL MARKET PATIO

The Texas-based gourmet grocer's serpentine-flow layout, with its acres of produce, hundreds of cheeses, and thousands of wines, is reason enough to visit. But it's the weekend live music on the open-air patio that's a must-do. Every Friday, Saturday, and sometimes Thursday and Sunday from mid-March through Halloween (weather permitting), live local bands take the stage for at least a three-hour set of toe-tapping tunes. The tradition has been going on since the store's first spring season in 2002, and band genres range from classic rock and country to '90s pop and rhythm and blues. The stage has hosted the likes of Grammy Award–winning Western swing band Asleep at the Wheel, Maren Morris, and Luke Wade. What's great is that customers can purchase a bottle of wine, some sushi, a cup of gelato, or whatever they want to create their own patio picnic. The playground is also a lifesaver for parents of little ones.

4651 West Freeway, 817-989-4700
www.centralmarket.com

GO TO A YEAR-ROUND RODEO AT COWTOWN COLISEUM

No need to wait for the Fort Worth Stock Show & Rodeo in January. Rodeos happen every Friday and Saturday night in the heart of the Fort Worth Stockyards inside the century-old Cowtown Coliseum. Built in 1908, the historic structure—with its dirt-filled arena and rugged, authentically Western atmosphere—draws amateur and professional athletes locally and from across the country. Rodeo events range from team roping and barrel racing to bull riding and calf scrambles for the kids. (Sign your little buckaroo up to participate upon entry.) Note that the Texas Rodeo Cowboy Hall of Fame occupies the coliseum's corridors, so plan extra time to peruse. Also keep your eyes peeled for celeb sightings. A visit by Prince Harry, Duke of Sussex, in 2022 has all eyes on this Fort Worth tradition.

121 E Exchange Ave., 1-888-COWTOWN
www.cowtowncoliseum.com

TIP

Watch the calendar for occasional matinee rodeos.

40

PACK A PICNIC
FOR CONCERTS IN THE GARDEN

There are many great ways to spend a Texas summer night, and this ranks near the very top. The Fort Worth Symphony Orchestra's outdoor concert series, held on the soft, grassy lawn of the Fort Worth Botanic Garden in June through July 4, is like the Super Bowl of picnics. Many attendees make it a tradition to break out their very best in portable food and drink, from jumbo shrimp cocktail to top-shelf margaritas shaken on-site. A limited menu of food, beer, and wine is sold at the show, but it's more fun to showcase your picnic-packing skills—so splurge on that nice charcuterie platter and maybe even some caviar. Note that there are tickets for table seats and the lawn, and the latter fills quickly upon the gates opening.

Fort Worth Botanic Garden
3220 Botanic Garden Blvd., 817-463-4160
www.fwbg.org

Fort Worth Symphony Orchestra, 817-665-6000
www.fwsymphony.org

TIP

Pack a hand-held fan as the heat is usually sweltering, but only until the sun goes down. Also, don't forget dessert for the post-concert fireworks show.

TAKE A ROOFTOP TOUR

OF FORT WORTH SKYLINE VIEWS

The city's rooftop bar scene is growing, and the breathtaking views alone are worth a multi-stop tour. On the list is Ático, chef Tim Love's Spanish-inspired rooftop tapas bar in the Springhill Suites Stockyards. The nearly 360-degree panorama comes with luxe lounge seating, an open kitchen, hors d'oeuvres, and cocktails. Lot 12 is the Horned Frog fan's hottest hangout, located atop the Hyatt Place Fort Worth/TCU. The indoor–outdoor rooftop terrace bar provides a bird's-eye view of the university grounds, beautiful nearby neighborhoods, and downtown in the distance. For upscale Mexican food, don't miss the rooftop patio and bar at Tinie's. The second-story, string-lit deck provides twinkling views of the city lights. Back downtown, the chic Sinclair Hotel takes guests to grand heights atop its 17th-floor luxury rooftop bar. Grab a seat at the sleek white bar for a cocktail and enjoy star-speckled skies.

Ático
2315 N Main St., 682-255-5112
www.aticoftworth.com

Lot 12
2512 W Berry St., 817-353-2344
www.lot12tcu.com

Tinie's
113 S Main St., 682-255-5425
www.tiniesfw.com

The Sinclair
512 Main St., 682-231-8124
www.thesinclairhotel.com

SEE A CONCERT
AT DICKIES ARENA

In 2019, when it was announced that George Strait would play one of the very first concerts at the brand new Dickies Arena, the caliber of potential performers that could now tour through Fort Worth was realized. Cowtown finally had a venue that could draw big names, from Paul McCartney and Parker McCollum to Eric Clapton and Eric Church. Dickies and its 14,000 seats have also hosted big national events, from US Olympic Team trials to NCAA basketball tournaments. The arena boasts the nation's second-largest continuous 360-degree center screen, making every seat a great one. Don't miss the two magnificent glass tile mosaic murals under each of the building's two main entrances. Each was commissioned specifically for the arena and to showcase Fort Worth's Western heritage with Texas flora, fauna, cowhands, and caballos—which means "horses" in Spanish.

1911 Montgomery St., 817-402-9000
www.dickiesarena.com

43

LOOK UP AT THE CEILING
AT WHITE ELEPHANT SALOON

Neatly nailed in rows on the ceiling and walls of this iconic Stockyards bar are several dozen well-worn cowboy hats. The White Elephant Saloon goes back to the 1890s, and while its current location opened in the 1970s, Fort Worth's authentic Western roots are apparent upon entry. Order a longneck and find a seat at the brass-railed wooden bar—it's easy to sit and stay awhile. First, there are the hats to peruse; each one's donor is noted with a name plate. Next, meander to the glass cases along the wall behind the bar to see hundreds of white elephant figurines gifted to the saloon over the years. Most importantly, take in the daily live music, two-stepping couples on the small but sturdy wooden dance floor, and the diversity of the crowd—from bright-eyed international tourists to locals ordering their usuals.

106 E Exchange Ave., 817-624-8273
www.whiteelephantsaloon.com

BET ON THE CADDIE RACES

AT COLONIAL'S 13TH HOLE

When the PGA Tour makes its annual stop in Fort Worth in late May, everyone in town becomes a golf fan. Colonial Country Club becomes Fort Worth's hottest destination, where the Colonial National Invitation (titled differently for various sponsors throughout the years) hosts some of the PGA's biggest names along with a festive scene that makes the quiet game of golf downright exciting. Part of that scene is the 13th hole, the course's shortest but perhaps most challenging hole, which is guarded by a lake coming in from the right and two bunkers on the left. It's nicknamed "the party hole," and spectators here have made it a tradition to bet on which golfer's caddie will arrive to the green first. Although sometimes frowned upon by PGA officials and golf purists, the tradition hasn't died, and cheers can be heard from around the course. It's a spectacle worth witnessing, cold beer in hand and perhaps a wager in the other.

3735 Country Club Cir., 817-927-4200
www.colonialfw.com

Photo credit: Colonial Country Club

45

CELEBRATE LOCAL ART
AT ARTSGOGGLE

What started as the Near Southside's own version of an indoor gallery night in 2003 has grown to spill out onto the streets, boasting more than a mile of artists' booths along West Magnolia Avenue. The one-day only event draws 60,000-plus for food, drinks, live music, and performances along with artistic displays as diverse as the district itself. Consider this art festival the people's festival, as all featured artists (around 1,000 of them) are local, with virtually no applicant being turned away. This means aspiring artists have a chance to display and sell their work alongside tenured professionals—so keep your eyes peeled for the next masterpiece.

W Magnolia Ave. and Near Southside District, 817-923-1649
www.artsgoggle.org

Snag patio or streetside seating early at one of the many culinary hot spots on West Magnolia Avenue, such as Nonna Tata or Ellerbe Fine Foods. ArtsGoggle provides for epic people-watching, especially with a glass of wine in hand.

STAY THE NIGHT IN A SHIPPING CONTAINER
AT HOTEL OTTO

"Otto" means "eight" in Italian, and that's how many 160-square-foot bungalows combine to comprise Hotel Otto, a micro-resort from restaurateur and chef Tim Love. The destination sits snugly next to Love's Italian restaurant Gemelle, meaning delicious dinner, drinks, and even breakfast are located just a few steps away. Each tiny home is constructed from one cargo container and features a rooftop patio with lounge seating and a firepit. Luxe amenities inside include a cushy queen-sized bed (your suitcase will fit underneath), Hermes bath products, an Illy espresso machine, and a complimentary bar set-up for crafting your own Aperol spritz—the restaurant's signature cocktail. Stick around for "knocktails" at 5 p.m., when a friendly bartender will knock on your door, complimentary libations in tow.

4400 White Settlement Rd., 833-4OTTOFW
www.hotelottoftw.com

TIP
All bungalows sit close to one another, providing perfect accommodations for a group overnight stay with a multi-rooftop patio party.

47

LISTEN TO AN ACOUSTIC SET IN A 1940s POST OFFICE

AT THE POST AT RIVER EAST

Lots of bars and patios in town offer live music, but the list of intimate music venues with ticketed performances is much smaller. A must-visit standout is The Post at River East, located in the shell of a former 1946 post office just east of downtown. Acoustic performances take place almost daily outside on the string-lit courtyard, and the dimly-lit 2,000 square-foot interior features a red curtained stage for ticketed shows. With a primary focus on Americana, artists here have ranged from Radney Foster and Tommy Alverson to Chris Knight and Sunny Sweeney. Patrons can expect a casual yet sophisticated atmosphere (no mosh pits here) with professional service. Lunch and dinner are served, too. Think pulled-pork nachos, ham and brie sandwiches, and "cowboy" hummus with black-eyed peas.

2925 Race St., 817-945-8890
www.thepostatrivereast.com

Photo credit: The Post at River East

48

BUY ONE NEW PIECE FROM AN ARTIST EVERY YEAR

AT MAIN STREET FORT WORTH ARTS FESTIVAL

For four days in April, downtown Fort Worth is home to the largest and most spectacular festival in the Southwest, featuring a feast of cuisine, more than 80 musical acts, and world-class art. A quick reminder for those who've been: Of the more than 1,000 artist applicants from across the country, only 200 are selected. This means every highly coveted artist booth will showcase something truly special, be it photographic prints, beach glass jewelry, leather goods, or one-of-a-kind yard sculptures. There's also an Emerging Artists section featuring more than 20 local artists who are first-time exhibitors. Show up hungry (and thirsty) for delicious food that goes well beyond typical festival fare. (Don't miss the Bavarian crème puff.) Also, go early—the artist booths close around sunset, but the live music stays on until well after dark.

817-336-2787
www.mainstreetartsfest.org

LAUGH UNTIL IT HURTS
AT A FOUR DAY WEEKEND IMPROV COMEDY SHOW

Discover the hysterical art of improv comedy as performed by some of the industry's best, right in downtown Fort Worth. Four Day Weekend launched in 1997, and the comedy troupe has been drawing crowds for belly laughs ever since. The entire show is audience driven, meaning guests get to choose much of the comedic content. For example, attendees are asked to write a topic on a Post-It note prior to the show from which the comedians may randomly choose for a comical segment. Or the audience may post a photo on Facebook during the show, which could be chosen as the subject for another segment. The result is an unbelievable sequence of comedic relief that's as funny as it is impromptu. A Four Day Weekend show is a sure bet for birthday gatherings, date nights, corporate outings, or anytime general merriment is needed.

312 Houston St., 817-226-4329
www.fourdayweekend.com

CATCH SKY-HIGH VIEWS
ATOP THE FERRIS WHEEL AT MAYFEST

The towering Ferris wheel is just one of many traditions to experience at this annual, four-day, family-friendly festival, which has been held across 33 acres in Trinity Park every May for more than five decades. At the wheel's peak at 66 feet high, have your camera ready to capture downtown skyline views and cotton candy clouds—both reflect off the Trinity River like a mirror. Back at ground level, partake in festival food, live music, and an art and gift market, or simply people-watch on the lawn. All children's activities (more than 20 of them) are free, so prepare to wear out the little ones with arts and crafts, a mini maze, a giant sand pit, and entertainment on the Children's Performing Arts Stage. Mayfest all but guarantees a quiet ride home and a good night's sleep.

Trinity Park, 2401 University Dr., 817-332-1055
www.mayfest.org

51

CATCH A DOUBLE FEATURE
AT COYOTE DRIVE-IN

With four screens, a food and beverage pavilion that serves beer and wine, and a kids' play area, Coyote Drive-In is one of the country's premier drive-in movie theaters. As part of Panther Island, the attraction is worth a visit if only for the sunset views of downtown Fort Worth along the Trinity River. Note that cars line up early to get a good spot, and each screen will show two movies for just one ticket price. Clean out the truck bed and pack the lawn chairs. Dogs are welcome, too! But leave the outside food and drinks at home, because the Canteen's lengthy menu and bar is open early and late through the end of all flicks.

223 NE 4th St., 817-717-7767
www.coyotedrive-in.com/fortworth

TIP

If you have a large group, contact the drive-in in advance to check on potential discount pricing.

52

DRINK BEER FROM A STEIN
AT OKTOBERFEST FORT WORTH

Recognized nationally as one of the top Oktoberfest festivals in the country, Oktoberfest Fort Worth draws thousands over three days for a celebration of German food, music, and culture. It takes place in late September at Panther Island along the Trinity River, with most of the activity happening in the covered pavilion and under big tents. There are multiple stages for live polka music and plenty of room for dancing. Go hungry for schnitzel, sausage, potato pancakes, Bavarian pretzels, strudel, and more. Wash it all down with a tall German beer poured in a heavy stein glass that's yours to keep. When the liquid courage sets in, try your hand (and arm) at the stein-hoisting competition—one of several contests that range from barrel rolling races to the Dachshund dash.

395 Purcey St., 817-698-0700
www.oktoberfestfw.com

GALLERY HOP
ON GALLERY NIGHT

Twice a year—in the spring and fall—dozens of local art galleries, museums, and studios come alive after dark for Gallery Night, hosted by the Fort Worth Art Dealers Association. Patrons stroll through participating destinations, many who offer light bites, wine, and in some cases a live musician. Nearby restaurants and retail businesses also often participate by displaying artists' works. Venues are mostly located along Camp Bowie Boulevard, although the map of participants reaches as far as Arlington. Michaels Cuisine and Winslow's Wine Café are both popular Gallery Night "starter spots" for dinner, so make reservations early, or visit for a post gallery nightcap. The event showcases Fort Worth's thriving artist community in a fun way that's great for a group outing, too.

www.fwada.com/gallerynight

54

GET A WEEKENDER PASS

TO THE FORT WORTH FOOD + WINE FESTIVAL

It's the ultimate way to experience the annual four-day culinary taste of Fort Worth, where the city's top chefs, restaurants, breweries, and distilleries showcase their delicious best. The Weekender Pass gets you access to all six events, held day and night at various venues around town, with early entry and VIP perks. Events range from Tacos + Tequila and the dessert-centric Nite Bites to Burgers, Brews + Blues. Break out the stretchy pants and prepare for a marathon of eating and drinking. If the Weekender Pass is too hard on the pocketbook, visiting any one of the festival's events a la carte is still a Fort Worth must. Proceeds benefit the Fort Worth Food + Wine Foundation, which raises funds for local grant programs and culinary scholarships.

www.fortworthfoodandwinefestival.com

TIP

The Weekender Pass typically sells out weeks in advance, so plan on purchasing early.

55

RESERVE A FRONT-ROW SEAT

FOR THE FORT WORTH PARADE OF LIGHTS

An up-close street-side view is a game-changer for this annual Christmas event, which draws thousands to downtown Fort Worth. There are usually around 100 twinkling floats from local organizations all across Tarrant County, and a front-row seat ensures that you'll be able to see them all. (Otherwise, plan to tiptoe to peer over the heads of everyone standing in front of you.) Tickets go on sale a couple months beforehand, and the parade is typically held the Sunday before Thanksgiving. Plan to arrive downtown no later than 4 p.m. to beat the traffic funneling in, and grab dinner at a downtown restaurant. For even more festive fun, search for seats by one of the parade announcers for an entertaining float-by-float rundown.

Downtown Fort Worth, 817-336-2787
www.fortworthparadeoflights.org

SEE THE NUTCRACKER
AT BASS PERFORMANCE HALL

It's a Christmastime tradition for folks of all ages to get dressed up and head downtown to visit the world-renowned performance space for the annual season of The Nutcracker. Performed by Fort Worth–based Texas Ballet Theater, the show follows the classic storyline of Clara and her Nutcracker Prince traveling through a winter wonderland to meet the Sugar Plum Fairy in the Kingdom of Sweets via dancers in exquisite costumes executing mesmerizing choreography. Elegant Christmas trees line Bass Hall's lobby windows and serve as twinkling backdrops for family photos before and after the show. The hall's exterior trumpet-playing angels only add to the holiday magic. Plan on purchasing a souvenir nutcracker to take home. Or visit any time of year during one of Bass Hall's many Broadway shows or concerts featuring prestigious acts.

525 Commerce St., 817-212-4280
www.basshall.com

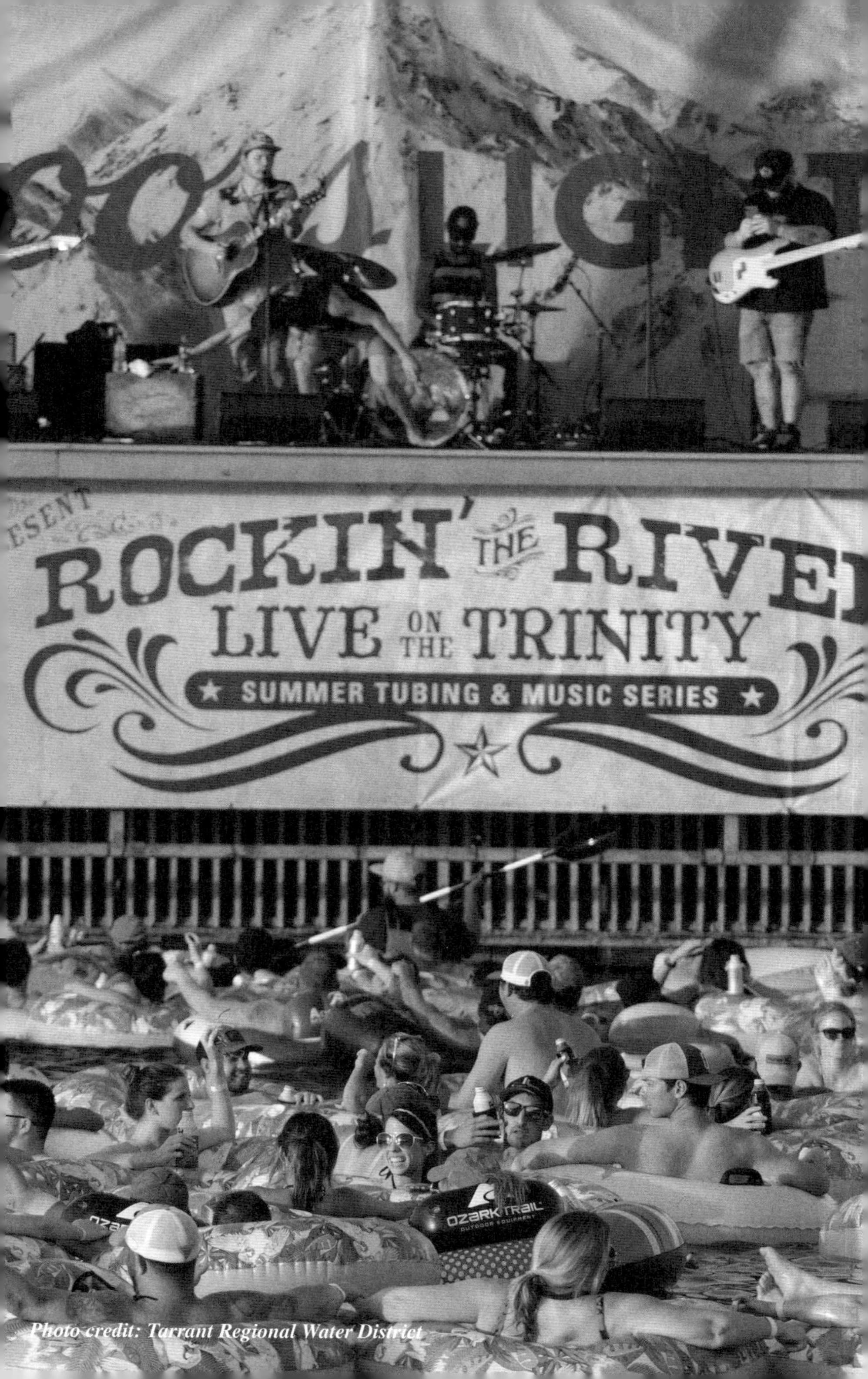

ROCKIN' THE RIVER
LIVE ON THE TRINITY
★ SUMMER TUBING & MUSIC SERIES ★

Photo credit: Tarrant Regional Water District

OUTDOORS AND RECREATION

57

HIT A PATIO AFTER A WALK OR JOG

ON THE TRINITY TRAILS

There's about a two- to three-mile stretch along the Trinity River where walkers, joggers, and cyclists can choose from several restaurant patios to stop and stretch their legs. Press Café, Woodshed Smokehouse, HG Sply Co., and Ascension Coffee all sit directly on the trails, each with festive patio seating areas that provide waterfront views and great people-watching, especially on a sunny Saturday. Press Café offers two levels of seating, with mimosas and brunch dishes that beckon. HG Sply Co. takes a healthy but hearty take on its meals, with cocktails that don't disappoint. Ascension Coffee is known for just that—high-quality coffees, lattes, and espresso with a small menu of interesting, Australian-inspired breakfast dishes. Yet nothing quite beats a cold beer and brisket tacos paired with live music on the Woodshed Smokehouse patio—get there early to get a seat. With new development a constant, more establishments along the trails are no doubt on the way.

Ascension Coffee
1751 River Run, 817-865-3829
www.ascension.coffee

HG Sply Co.
1621 River Run, 682-730-6070
www.hgsplyco.com

Press Café
4801 Edwards Ranch Rd., 817-570-6002
www.presscafeftworth.com

Woodshed Smokehouse
3201 Riverfront Dr., 817-877-4545
www.woodshedsmokehouse.com

PLAY GOLF AFTER DARK
AT BENBROOK PAR 3

No collared shirt required at this friendly, unpretentious, nine-hole golf course, which features short holes and expansive views right next to breezy Benbrook Lake. Distances range between 62 and 177 yards, good for golfers looking to work on their short game and for beginners just learning to play and hit the green—or the ball, for that matter. Even more, the course is lit, so the fun can continue well after dark. There's also a driving range and an 18-hole mini-golf course that's been operating since 1977. Newer is the private event space and covered patios, both great for group events and parties. Golf carts are available for rent, as are clubs. Don't be hesitant to bring the kids. You just might start a tradition that creates an appreciation for the game, or at least fond memories that last a lifetime.

1801 Winscott Rd., 817-249-4653
www.benbrookgolf.com

59

FIND YOUR INNER WESTERN SPIRIT

WITH A HORSEBACK TRAIL RIDE

While Fort Worth is nicknamed "Cowtown," horses may be more prevalent around town than cattle. (Even the Fort Worth Police Department has a mounted patrol unit.) Travel the city as pioneers did by saddling up on a beautiful equine for a leisurely trail ride. At Stockyards Stables, riders can take a relaxing journey through the wooded Chisholm Trail to the Trinity River, where they are greeted with grassy fields and downtown skyline views. Or head southwest to Benbrook Stables, where trails wind around scenic Benbrook Lake, often through grasslands full of wildflowers or even hidden creeks. Both venues offer 30-minute or one-hour rides, and both are open seven days a week. Be sure to check age requirements and weight restrictions in advance.

Benbrook Stables, 10001 Benbrook Blvd., 817-249-1001
www.benbrookstables.com

Stockyards Stables, 157 E Exchange Ave., 817-247-2510
www.fortworthstockyardsstables.com

RUN THE COWTOWN
IN THE COLD

The annual multi-race event—the largest in North Texas—takes place rain, sleet, snow, or shine every year in late February, and while conditions are often frigid, that doesn't stop thousands of runners from bundling up to participate. Whether you walk the 5K or train for the marathon, there's an option for folks of all capabilities. Race routes wind through various scenic attractions and landmarks in Fort Worth, from the Cultural District and downtown to the Trinity River trails and the Fort Worth Stockyards. End at the festive post-race expo for hydration, refueling, and recovery with food, drinks, music, and entertainment. Prefer not to race? If you're local with a home on the marathon race route (or know someone who is), set up a cheering station to give runners some motivation—with mimosas all around.

2617 Whitmore St., 817-207-0224
www.cowtownmarathon.org

WATCH A CONCERT

FROM AN INNER-TUBE AT ROCKIN' THE RIVER

Grab an inner tube and get in—the water's just fine. Hosted by the Tarrant Regional Water District at Panther Island Pavilion, Rockin' the River is a summer concert series where spectators float their way to the stage. Typically held in July and August, the series features notable Texas country and Red Dirt acts who perform on Texas's only waterfront stage, which is 50 feet wide and sits right on the Trinity River. The series celebrated its 10th anniversary in 2021 and draws from folks far and wide—a few thousand each weekend. Back on dry land, concert-goers can catch rays on the sandy beach or grassy lawn, grab a bite from local food vendors, or sip a cold beer at the pavilion bar. All floaters are required to leave the water by sunset, but that's when a second show begins on the lawn stage followed by one explosive fireworks display.

395 Purcey St., 817-698-0700
www.rockintheriverfw.com

62

HIT THE TOWN ON TWO WHEELS

WITH FORT WORTH BIKE SHARING

Rentals from this city-wide bike share system can span an hour or more, but a short ride is all you need to experience the fun and convenience of the program. There are bike dock stations all over, from downtown, the Cultural District, and the Trinity Trails to the Near Southside, Stockyards, and Texas Christian University. Simply swipe a credit card and unload your bike, then return it to a station when your ride is complete. Some folks use the system for commuting to work or school, while others ride for leisure or to explore the city. Don't miss the newer electric bikes available at some stations—great for swiftly climbing those hills with ease. Most of the bikes have handlebar baskets, so pack a lunch or a snack for trailside pit stops.

817-215-8600, www.fortworthbikesharing.com

PLAY BEACH VOLLEYBALL
AT TWIN POINTS PARK

A retreat to the beach is just 15 miles from downtown Fort Worth thanks to Twin Points Park, located in a beautifully maintained southern portion of Eagle Mountain Lake. While Twin Points has been a destination for its lakefront swimming hole and sandy beaches for decades, the park was completely revamped and improved in 2012 when the Tarrant Regional Water District became not only the owner of the property, but the operator as well. Today, there are several covered pavilions with charcoal grills for cooking out, green spaces and picnic tables, shady trees for meandering, and plenty of beach area for lounging under an umbrella or partaking in a friendly game of beach volleyball, long popular here. Also look for beach yoga classes and paddleboard rentals.

10200 Ten Mile Bridge Rd., 817-720-4551
www.twinpointspark.com

KAYAK OR CANOE THE TRINITY RIVER

Experience how tranquil Fort Worth can be from the waters of the Trinity River. While there are multiple entry points for launching a kayak or canoe, start with Panther Island Pavilion. Here Backwoods Paddlesports can help anyone new to paddling with not only rentals but also a quick overview on the sport. Once outfitted, paddlers can enter via the free public beach and choose from three routes, ranging from a quarter-mile to five and a half miles. All three routes provide calm flows and scenic views. Expect to see lots of turtles and birds. Note that Backwoods Paddlesports is open seasonally. Other popular launch points on the river include West Fork at the White Settlement Trailhead (there's parking and restroom facilities here), and West Fork at Beach Street, home to the Fort Worth Rowing Club. And don't worry about a little water—your bottom is supposed to get wet.

480 N Taylor St., 817-470-2613
www.backwoodspaddlesports.com

LIVE LIFE IN THE FAST LANE
AT ROCKWOOD GO-KARTS

It's Fort Worth's oldest—and fastest—go-cart track, and it celebrated its 60th anniversary in 2022. Racers can reach speeds up to 20 to 30 miles per hour in a single-seat or two-seat go-cart. While rides are short—only four minutes—the adrenaline rush starts the moment your foot hits the pedal. After the ride, have your picture taken at the winner's circle stand, then wind down with an 18-hole game of mini-golf, also located on-site. But be prepared for challenges—this is not the basic flat course of the past. From clearing narrow bridges to jumping small streams, the impressively manicured course provides a crafty new test with every hole. Go early or stay after dark, as the destination is open seven days a week until late at night.

700 N University Dr., 817-626-1913
www.rockwoodgokarts.com

SPOT THE ALLIGATORS AT THE FORT WORTH NATURE CENTER & REFUGE

Alligators in Fort Worth aren't a myth. The large reptiles have been spotted more than once in area waters, particularly in the wetlands of the 3,600-acre Fort Worth Nature Center & Refuge. While sightings are rare, those documented with photos reveal gators up to 10 feet in length. In fact, park officials estimate that 50–100 alligators reside in the Nature Center, although the numbers vary by season and by the gators' own cannibalism, shockingly enough. The park is also home to forests, prairies, roaming bison, unique birds, and stretches of water that provide for some really good crappie fishing. (No bank fishing allowed.) Whether perusing the 20 miles of shady hiking trails or boating the calm and winding section of Lake Worth located within the park, keep your eyes peeled and your camera ready.

9601 Fossil Ridge Rd., 817-392-7410
www.fwnaturecenter.org

67

FIND FIVE MINUTES OF PEACE
AT THE FORT WORTH WATER GARDENS

Amid the concrete jungle that is downtown Fort Worth lies a tranquil oasis. The Fort Worth Water Gardens is an urban park designed by Philip Johnson (who also designed the Amon Carter Museum of American Art) hidden below terraced knolls, where multiple pools provide for a calming and rejuvenating experience. The gardens' signature feature is the cascading active pool, where steps lead to almost 40 feet below ground level. The powerful sound of flowing water surrounds those who venture to the bottom, drowning out city noise from above at street level. There's also a reflecting pool that sits below 22-foot walls. Both are perfect places to sit with a cup of coffee or lunch to-go. Put away the phone, and take in the serene surroundings.

1502 Commerce St., 817-392-7111
www.fortworthtexas.gov/departments/parks/
parks-and-trails/water-gardens

BOWL A STRIKE
AT COWTOWN BOWLING PALACE

Less about flash and more about nostalgia, this classic bowling alley has been around since 1957, making it a must-visit for generations. It's frequented by bowling league pros as much as families looking for a rainy-day activity and has always offered affordable entertainment. Inside, colorful print carpet and brightly checkered floor tile provide for a festive atmosphere. But things really get exciting during "cosmic bowling," when the lights are turned down and special effect lighting comes on along with jamming music. Save room for the snack bar, which offers far more than snacks. Menu items range from breakfast platters, burgers, and pizza to fried pickles, wings, and chicken strip baskets. Wash it all down with a cold pitcher of beer. Bring the kids, too. There are bumpers that easily raise for their turn.

4333 River Oaks Blvd., 817-624-2151
www.cowtownbowling.com

PEDAL YOUR OWN MOBILE BAR
WITH COWTOWN CYCLE PARTY

Load up 8 to 16 of your best friends and tour downtown from this mobile pedal party, where riders work in tandem to cruise the streets. The Cowtown Cycle Party is basically a moving bar on wheels, where riders pedal together to gain speeds from about five to eight miles per hour. The more people pedaling, the faster (and easier) it moves. Barstools serve as bike seats, elbows and BYOB beverages can rest on a wooden bar, and the entire apparatus is covered and adorned with longhorn steer horns at the front. A provided driver (who works for tips) steers the vehicle and can direct patrons to hot spots around downtown and the Near Southside. Pit stops at bars or cool landmarks are common, and rides are typically booked for two hours—although more time may be added. The cycle party is great for family reunions, bachelorette and birthday parties, corporate outings, or just spending a sunny afternoon outside.

129 Leuda St., 682-422-9253
www.cowtowncycleparty.com

STEP DOWN THE ROSE RAMP

AT THE FORT WORTH BOTANIC GARDEN

While there are 25 different garden spaces located within the Fort Worth Botanic Garden, the Rose Garden is perhaps the most iconic. It was completed in 1933—a year before the Fort Worth Botanic Garden was established—and built with 4,000 tons of Texas sandstone to create multiple levels of blooming beauty. Start at the top of the Rose Ramp, where the open-air Shelter House sits high above the Lower Rose Garden and Reflection Pond, then walk down stone steps amid rose flowerbeds that frame a cascading waterfall. The Rose Garden is one of the most beautiful and romantic spots in Fort Worth (many proposals and weddings take place here) and is listed on the National Register of Historic Places.

3220 Botanic Garden Blvd., 817-463-4160
www.fwbg.org

TAKE A DIP
IN BURGER'S LAKE

Tucked away in a hidden, wooded corner of town is a one-acre spring-fed swimming hole that's been serving up sandy beaches, sunshine, and nostalgia for generations. Astonishingly open since 1929, Burger's Lake draws folks by the car-full who line up upon opening to grab a picnic table and perhaps a charcoal grill to spend the day. Water features have grown over the decades, today including multiple diving boards, waterslides, and even a 25-foot trapeze attraction. Towering trees provide shade while spring-fed water keeps the lake crisp and cool. Outside picnics are permitted, but alcohol is not. There's also a menu of concessions available in the park, including onion rings, pizza slices, snow cones, and of course, burgers. Note that operating hours are from Memorial Day weekend through Labor Day weekend.

1200 Meandering Rd., 817-737-3414
www.burgerslake.com

SLOW DOWN TIME
WITH A RIDE ON THE FOREST PARK MINIATURE RAILROAD

Whether entertaining kids or not, a ride on this mid-20th Century miniature train is a nostalgic must for folks of all ages. It's believed to be the longest park train in the country and was recognized by the *Guinness Book of World Records* for just that when it opened in 1959. With its seven coaches and room for around 100 passengers, the train makes a five-mile roundtrip loop over the Trinity River and through the woods of Trinity Park, all while patrons sit back and take in the scenic views. Perhaps the most exciting part is the trip over a narrow bridge that crosses high above the Trinity River, which happens twice since the train makes a U-turn at the halfway point. So whether you take a camera or a good book, settle into a slower pace—for about 40 minutes at least. Bring cash, as no other forms of payment are accepted.

1700 Colonial Pkwy., 817-966-5509
www.forestparktrains.com

WITNESS THE WATERFALL
AT MARION SANSOM PARK

Referred to as simply Sansom Park by locals, this expansive wooded area boasts several interconnecting loops of hidden, winding trails on an incline, making it very popular for hikers and mountain bikers. At the top there are scenic views of lush green treetops and shimmery Lake Worth. Those who venture to the bottom are greeted by a lengthy waterfall, located a few yards below Lake Worth's dam. Dip your toes in to cool off or bring a rod and reel to cast a few. Some bring a picnic to share on a log, while others might keep moving to explore all 11 miles of trails. Located just 15 minutes north of downtown, the park is free to enter. Dogs on leashes are welcome, too. Don't forget your water bottle and camera to capture the calming scenery.

2501 Roberts Cut Off Rd., 817-392-5700
www.fortworthtexas.gov/departments/parks/parks-and-trails/marion-sansom-park

TAKE A SPIN
AROUND PANTHER ISLAND ICE

For about two months out of the year—from mid-November to mid-January—Panther Island invites guests to experience a bit of winter magic with its real ice-skating rink. Located under a large outdoor pavilion, the rink is protected from the elements and provides for some frozen fun seven days a week, regardless of Texas weather. Skating slots are booked in 75-minute increments, so there's always plenty of room to strut your stuff—or simply practice staying upright. A full menu, including beer and wine, is provided by neighboring Coyote Drive-In. There's also plenty of parking and covered seating with heaters. Dress appropriately—tall socks and gloves are recommended. Note that skating tickets aren't required for family members who just wish to watch.

223 NE 4th St., 682-704-7711
www.pantherislandice.com

75

SEE THE WORLD'S LARGEST HDTV
AT TEXAS MOTOR SPEEDWAY

Spanning a half-acre in size at nearly 23,000 square feet, "Big Hoss" is Texas Motor Speedway's massive high-definition scoreboard. The Guinness Book of World Records recognized the 108-ton structure as the world's largest TV prior to the April 2014 Cup race. To put this in perspective, the TV stands 12 stories high and is 79 percent larger than the behemoth video board at AT&T Stadium, home of the Dallas Cowboys. While Big Hoss is certainly something to see, so is the speedway itself. Opened in 1997, the stadium accommodates 200,000 fans and hosts all three NASCAR national series as well as the NTT IndyCar Series among various races and specialty events throughout the year. Experience the speedway like die-hard fans and plan a camping trip around a weekend race. The speedway can accommodate Class A motor homes to family tents.

3545 Lone Star Cir., 817-215-8500
www.texasmotorspeedway.com

WELCOME A NEWBORN
AT THE FORT WORTH ZOO

There must be something in the water at the Fort Worth Zoo, which snagged number one on the list of *USA Today's* 10 Best Zoos in North America in 2020. A big bundle of joy seems to arrive every few years, ranging from baby elephants, a gorilla, and a giraffe to a zebra, a jaguar, a rhino, and more. Catching a glimpse of these brand-new sweet creatures frolicking around their habitats—with their mothers in close proximity—is worth navigating through the crowds. Watch for the latest birth news via the giant billboard outside the Zoo's entrance at Colonial Parkway and South University Drive. In the meantime, visit 365 days a year to view more than 500 animal species, including more than 60 that are endangered and threatened.

1989 Colonial Pkwy., 817-759-7555
www.fortworthzoo.org

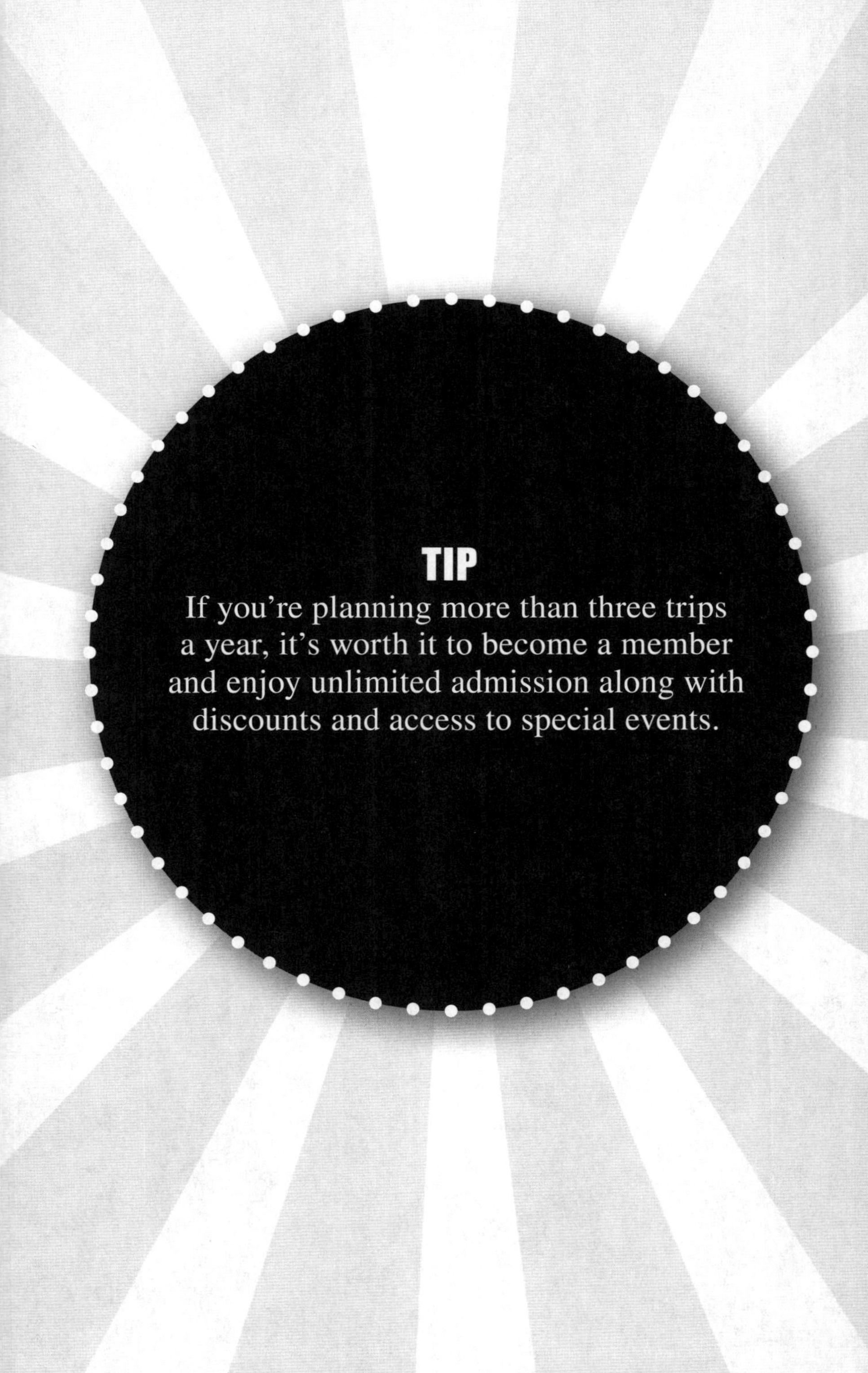
TIP
If you're planning more than three trips a year, it's worth it to become a member and enjoy unlimited admission along with discounts and access to special events.

Photo credit: The Foundry District

CULTURE AND HISTORY

77

TAKE A TRIP BACK IN TIME
AT LEONARD'S DEPARTMENT STORE MUSEUM

In 1918, a Fort Worth man named Marvin Leonard opened a small store that sold groceries and a few other goods. His brother Obie soon joined him in the venture and Leonard's Department Store was born. It was a superstore before there were superstores, one that eventually covered more than six city blocks in downtown Fort Worth. The store was so popular that families visited from miles away, some arriving via Leonard's own subway system, which shuttled customers in from a remote parking lot. At the Leonard's Department Store Museum, visitors can view actual merchandise and displays that appeared in the store, from clothing and cans of motor oil to a vintage cash register and a popcorn machine that provided complimentary freshly popped kernels to customers. Don't miss the Lionel electric train, which was first displayed in Leonard's "Toyland" department in 1955.

200 Carroll St., 817-336-9111
www.facebook.com/LeonardsMuseum

TIP

Bring the kids during the Christmas season to see Santa.

PEEK INSIDE HISTORIC HOMES

DURING THE RYAN PLACE CANDLELIT TOUR

As new home builds engulf the city at viral speed, historic neighborhoods like Ryan Place become even more precious. In 1979, Elizabeth Boulevard joined the National Register of Historic Places, making Ryan Place the only residential historic district in Fort Worth. Once a year the public can get an in-person look at what makes these early 20th century homes so majestic. During the two-day Christmastime tour, held the first weekend in December, visitors can purchase tickets to step inside a select list of historic homes, each dressed up in holiday regalia. From cattle barons' mansions to artistic bungalows, homes on the tour vary in architectural style. Along the way there's often live music, children's activities, and perhaps a food truck or two. The tour has raised hundreds of thousands for neighborhood projects, including the reconstruction of the stone entrance portals at 8th Avenue and Elizabeth Boulevard.

www.ryanplacefortworth.com/candlelight-tours

WITNESS THE WORLD'S
ONLY TWICE-DAILY CATTLE DRIVE

Led by real drovers clad in authentic 19th-century cowboy attire, a herd of actual Texas longhorns stroll the Stockyards daily at 11:30 a.m. and 4 p.m. along East Exchange Avenue. Spectators line the sidewalks—children atop parents' shoulders—to catch a glimpse of what is more like a leisurely promenade, not a stampede. These longhorns are of the docile, friendly breed, but do weigh in at anywhere from 1,400 to 2,500 pounds, with horns that measure six to nine feet tip to tip. (So stay on the sidewalks when the drovers ask you.) There is one longhorn in the herd for each decade of Fort Worth's past, and they are donated by area ranchers. The Fort Worth Herd was created as part of the city's sesquicentennial celebration in 1999.

129 E Exchange Ave., 817-336-4373
www.fortworth.com/the-herd/about-the-herd/

TIP
Catch a less-crowded weekday drive if you can, as the sidewalks fill quickly on the weekends.

RIDE IN A WORLD WAR II AIRCRAFT
AT THE VINTAGE FLYING MUSEUM

A close-up look at aviation history awaits you on Fort Worth's North Side thanks to the Vintage Flying Museum, which houses over a dozen historic aircraft in a massive hangar hidden from street view. Inside, folks will find World War II bomber planes and fighter jets along with notable aircraft like that owned by famed aviatrix Jackie Cochran, who set many records for women in flying. The museum doubles as a vintage aircraft mechanic's shop, as several dedicated and knowledgeable volunteers work regularly to maintain and upkeep these rare planes. Check the calendar of events for warbird ride days, where guests can book tickets for a plane ride that comes with a sky-high tour of town. Don't miss the Rosie the Riveter Memorial Rose Garden, located on-site to honor women who kept the country running as "Rosies" during World War II.

505 NW 38th St., 817-624-1935
www.vintageflyingmuseum.org

POSE FOR A PICTURE WITH A PIANIST

DURING THE VAN CLIBURN INTERNATIONAL PIANO COMPETITION

Once every four years "the Cliburn" rolls around, bringing with it a concert series featuring more than 170 music performances from exceptional pianists from all over the world and simultaneously launching the careers of many elite emerging artists. But these young competitors, ages 18 to 30, are already superstars upon their arrival, as witnessed by the droves of piano groupies that hang around the stage door after their performances at Bass Performance Hall. Join in to get an autograph and pose for a selfie. Any one of the performers might be a household name one day. Or, if you're local, take your support of the competition a step further by volunteering to provide transportation for the pianists or even hosting one in your own home.

201 Main St., 817-738-6536
www.cliburn.org

82

TAKE A GLASS BLOWING CLASS AT SINACA STUDIOS

Work with glass in its molten state at 2,100 degrees Fahrenheit at this South Fort Worth glass blowing studio, where both fledgling and tenured artists go to create one-of-a-kind pieces. The array of classes and workshops offered here is wide, but the two-hour glass blowing session in the hot shop is the most popular. Form and shape pieces like paperweights, small vases, and seasonal décor. Each participant gets to make at least two items. Note that glass blowing classes don't take place in July and August . . . Texas summers are just too hot. But there's also a cold working studio where folks can learn non-heated methods like wet belt sanding, wet tile sawing, and sand blasting. SiNaCa Studios sits in a repurposed vintage gas station where hundreds visit annually to learn the art of glass.

1013 W Magnolia Ave., 817-899-0024
www.sinacastudios.org

83

SEE THE WORLD'S SECOND-LONGEST BURNING LIGHTBULB

AT THE STOCKYARDS MUSEUM

Hidden inside the Livestock Exchange building is the Stockyards Museum, where exhibits include artifacts from the early days of the Stockyards. Amid collectibles such as saddles, spurs, Native American headdresses, and remnants from the Stockyards meat-packing industry is the Palace Theater Bulb, which has been burning since September 1908. Made by the now non-existent Shelby Electric Company, the softly lit bulb (which remains on a dimmer to preserve its power) was first installed at the Byers Opera House downtown, which later became the Palace Movie Theater. The theater was demolished in 1977, and the bulb eventually found its forever home in the Stockyards Museum. (Interestingly, the longest burning bulb lives at a firehouse in Livermore, California, and it, too, was made by Shelby Electric.) Museum guests can expect a birthday party for the bulb (often with cupcakes) on September 21 every year for as long as it burns.

131 E Exchange Ave., 817-625-5082
www.stockyardsmuseum.org

84

VISIT THE MODERN ART MUSEUM DURING A RAIN SHOWER

The Modern Art Museum's five, box-like gallery buildings shimmer against the shallow reflecting pond situated against them—almost like lanterns floating on water. Visit during a soft rain shower and witness raindrops dancing down the floor-to-ceiling glass windows onto the pond. It's a serene yet exhilarating way to experience building designer Tadao Ando's building architecture, which combines modern elements like concrete, glass, steel, and natural light. Inside there are nearly 3,000 works of modern and contemporary international art, including works by Andy Warhol, Japanese contemporary artist Takashi Murakami, and American abstract expressionist painter Lee Krasner. Don't miss dining at Café Modern, which provides stellar reflecting pond views and globally inspired comfort cuisine. Also a must is a movie at the Magnolia at the Modern, the museum's in-house theater featuring critically acclaimed films.

3200 Darnell St., 817-738-9215
www.themodern.org

85

MAIL A LETTER
AT THE HISTORIC DOWNTOWN POST OFFICE

One of the most architecturally spectacular indoor spaces in Fort Worth lies in the lobby of this historic landmark downtown, where, thanks to its elaborate beaux arts and classical revival design, the simple task of mailing a letter can feel like a regal experience. Built in 1933, the monumental building, with its 16 exterior limestone columns boasting Texas longhorn and Hereford cattle capitals, is listed on the National Register of Historic Places. While most might head to their designated neighborhood post office to send a package or buy stamps, the dramatic interior of this iconic structure is worth the trip downtown. Enter through the revolving door, which reveals green marble columns and intricate ceiling tilework throughout a lobby that runs the length of the entire building. Conveniently, the spacious parking lot always has open spots, and the line inside is rarely long.

251 W Lancaster Ave., 817-870-8128
www.dfwi.org/go/united-states-post-office-central

86

HAVE LUNCH
AT THE KIMBELL CAFÉ

The world-renowned art museum is home to the only Michelangelo in the Americas—*The Torment of Saint Anthony*—but it might be as popular for its lunch offerings as it is for its stunning exhibitions. The Kimbell's now-retired chef Shelby Shafer crafted a menu of mid-century soups, sandwiches, quiches, salads, and dreamy desserts that kept ladies who lunch (and their hungry husbands) coming back for more than 30 years. Her classic dishes still live on, alongside a few refreshed recipes. While the COVID-19 pandemic changed the restaurant format from buffet to café, patrons still get hearty portions of the Kimbell's elegant fare. Newer is the Kimbell Café's afternoon tea service, which offers scones, finger sandwiches, cookies, and muffins with house-made jams and butter. The Kimbell Café is located in the Louis I. Kahn Building, first opened to the public in 1972. With its barrel-vaulted porticos, the natural light-filled structure is still a mecca of modern architecture.

3333 Camp Bowie Blvd., 817-332-8451
www.kimbellart.org

87

EXPERIENCE THE BREADTH OF AMERICAN CREATIVITY

AT THE AMON CARTER MUSEUM OF AMERICAN ART

Admission is free at "The Carter," the fond nickname given to this Fort Worth Cultural District crown jewel of American art exhibitions. Inside is a visual timeline of American history through paintings and photography, from the sweeping landscape paintings of the 19th century and the urbanization of the 20th century to post–World War creativity and contemporary photography of today. Stories are told here without a word being said. It was philanthropist Amon G. Carter's vision that the museum be free for the people of Fort Worth. Carter died before the museum opened in 1961 but his daughter Ruth Carter Stevenson honored her father's legacy by acquiring the very best examples from various art genres. While the permanent collection is awe-inspiring, don't miss the culturally stimulating exhibitions.

3501 Camp Bowie Blvd., 817-738-1933
www.cartermuseum.org

BE AMAZED BY THE ANNIE OAKLEY HOLOGRAM

AT THE NATIONAL COWGIRL MUSEUM AND HALL OF FAME

Through the magic of hologram technology, Cowgirl Museum visitors can virtually meet Annie Oakley, the legendary sharpshooter who travelled the country with the Buffalo Bill Wild West Show as its only female performer. As part of the exhibit Hitting the Mark: Cowgirls and Wild West Shows, Annie spellbindingly shares her story as she reads her own handwritten letters, which are also on display along with her wedding ring and one of the shotguns used in her performing days. The Cowgirl is the only museum in the world dedicated to honoring women of the West. There are more than 4,000 artifacts and stories about more than 750 women, from pioneers to cowgirls of today. Country music fans, take note: Superstar Miranda Lambert was a 2021 inductee. And don't miss the gift shop, Desert Rose, on your way out.

1720 Gendy St., 817-336-4475
www.cowgirl.net

FOLLOW FORT WORTH'S HERITAGE TRAILS

There are approximately two dozen bronze plaques downtown detailing historic events that shaped Fort Worth's colorful history. Collectively they are called Heritage Trails—a history lesson provided by a leisurely walking path. Most of the plaques are positioned along Main Street, from the bronze depiction of The Wild Bunch—five outlaws including Butch Cassidy and the Sundance Kid—to the JFK Tribute, which commemorates President John F. Kennedy's impromptu speech to thousands downtown on November 22, 1963, with a bronze statue and famous quotes. "There are no faint hearts in Fort Worth," he said. The Heritage Trails feature everything from opera houses, grand hotels, "flying machines," and streetcars to architectural diversity, gamblers and gunfights, Hell's Half Acre, and the famous sleeping panther sculpture.

Downtown Fort Worth
www.fortworthheritagetrails.com

TAKE A PHOTO WITH "THE DUKE"

AT JOHN WAYNE: AN AMERICAN EXPERIENCE

The 10,000 square-foot exhibit, permanently located in the Fort Worth Stockyards, looks deeply into the life of Marion Mitchell Morrison, known worldwide to his fans as Western movie star John Wayne. Opened in 2020, the museum displays never-before-seen family photos, iconic film props, and even his dark green 1976 Grand Safari automobile. (Fun fact: Wayne had the roof raised on the vehicle so he wouldn't have to take off his cowboy hat upon entry.) The exhibit came to life when Wayne's son Ethan discovered just how much memorabilia his father had amassed. In the gallery "Life on Screen," guests are taken on a tour through his movie career, with the screenplay for the 1969 movie *True Grit* on display along with Wayne's Academy Award for Best Actor. But it's in the "America, Why I Love Her" gallery where guests get a glimpse of Wayne's personal life, patriotism, and love of ranching.

2501 Rodeo Plaza, 682-224-0956
www.johnwayne.com/experience

DIP YOUR OWN CANDLESTICKS

AT LOG CABIN VILLAGE

The living history museum provides a glimpse of 19th-century frontier living through a collection of Texas log cabins, some dating back to the mid- to late 1800s. There's a schoolhouse, a blacksmith shop, a grist mill, and six cabin homes. Historical interpreters in 19th-century clothing work to depict the lifestyle of those who lived in the structures. The Village is open year-round for visitors and field trip groups, who can watch blacksmith demos and even dip their own candles. Occasional Dutch-oven cooking demonstrations allow guests to see how pioneers made their meals in cast iron pots over fire. (Don't miss the hot samples.) Work began to establish the Village in the 1950s, when local historians realized log cabins and structures were rapidly vanishing from the Texas landscape. It opened to the public in 1966.

2100 Log Cabin Village, 817-392-5881
www.logcabinvillage.org

92

STUDY WESTERN ART
AT THE SID RICHARDSON MUSEUM

To examine the works of premier Western artists Frederic Remington and Charles M. Russell is to immerse oneself into the fierce reality that was the American West. Thanks to the late Fort Worth oilman and philanthropist Sid Richardson, one can do so for free at his namesake art museum. Located downtown in a 19th-century brick building on Main Street, the museum features Richardson's collection of more than 70 paintings by Remington and Russell, along with more from other notable Western artists. Don't miss *Buffalo Runners—Big Horn Basin*, an iconic Remington oil painting completed in 1909 depicting running horses in vivid color, or *Bucker*, a watercolor by Russell completed in 1897 showcasing a young, strapping cowboy aiming to tame a bucking bronco.

309 Main St., 817-332-6554
www.sidrichardsonmuseum.org

STROLL THE STOCKYARDS
ON A SATURDAY AFTERNOON

While most days are bustling in the Historic Fort Worth Stockyards, Saturdays showcase a phenomenally vibrant scene unlike anything in the country. From international tourists and locals to concert-goers, bar-hoppers, wedding parties, and professional rodeo contestants, patrons combing the cobblestone streets are as varied as chap designs on bull riders. Some might be shopping for boots while others are bringing their children to the petting zoo. Some might be dancing on the sidewalk to a country song playing from a bar, while others are sharing raw oysters and palomas on a patio. The recent addition of Mule Alley, a district of immaculately restored horse and mule barns, has only added to the booming scene with its collection of restaurants, shops, and entertainment venues. Grab a libation from an outdoor bar, sit on the grassy lawn outside Cowtown Coliseum for weekend live music, and don't forget to get a picture under the iconic Fort Worth Stockyards sign.

www.fortworthstockyards.org

www.mulealleyfortworth.com

TAKE A FORT WORTH MURAL TOUR

Cowtown has become a lot more colorful thanks to a recent art mural boom, one that's spreading north, south, east, and west from prominent districts to hidden side streets and alleyways. The outdoor displays range from modern abstract with bright colors and happy-go-lucky mottos (think "Dream on Dreamer" and "Good Vibes Only") to detailed exhibits showcasing Fort Worth's Western heritage. Murals can be found on Camp Bowie Boulevard, downtown, in the fledging Foundry District (where Inspiration Alley is touted as the largest outdoor gallery in Texas with more than 70 pieces of fine art), the Near Southside, the River District, River East, West Bend, the Trinity Trails, West 7th district, and more.

www.fortworth.com/things-to-do/murals

TIP
Check local community theater Amphibian Stage for an augmented reality tour of the Near Southside's public murals.

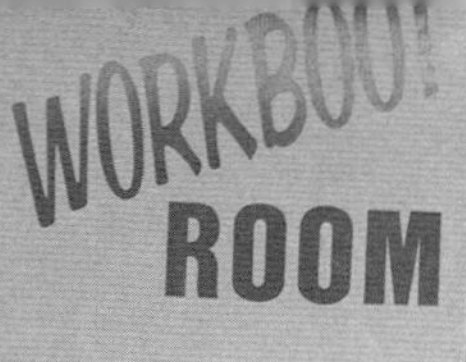

Photo credit: Justin Brands

SHOPPING AND FASHION

95

PUCKER UP
AT BEST MAID PICKLE EMPORIUM

Pickle lovers, rejoice. There's a store dedicated to all things pickle in the heart of Fort Worth. Hometown brand Best Maid dates back to 1926, when the company began selling its homemade mayonnaise. A sandwich spread soon followed that required pickle relish as an ingredient—hence, Best Maid pickles were born. At the Best Maid Pickle Emporium, customers are greeted by a giant-sized statue of Smiley, the Best Maid mascot—a little girl who's always smacking her lips. Shelf after shelf is fully stocked with shiny jars of jalapeno bread-and-butter pickles, kosher spears, baby dills, pickled okra, bloody-mary mix, and even green-hued, pickle-scented candles. Don't miss the timeline covering Best Maid's history in Fort Worth along with the video display on how pickles are made.

829 W Vickery Blvd., 682-351-8286
www.bestmaidpickles.com/pickle-emporium

CHRISTMAS SHOP
AT CHRISTMAS IN COWTOWN

There's one weekend in October where Fort Worth women far and wide (and a handful of men) can be found together in holiday shopping heaven: the Junior League of Fort Worth's Christmas in Cowtown Holiday Gift Market. The annual event overtakes the Amon G. Carter Jr. Exhibits Hall at Will Rogers Memorial Center for four days of frenzied shopping fueled by mimosas and credit cards. There are more than 200 merchants from across the country showcasing everything from monogrammed makeup bags and muffin mixes to furry rocking horses and fringed denim rompers. Folks will find this season's trends in every form, from baby gifts to home décor. There's a small fee for admission which goes toward the more than $5 million raised for local nonprofit agencies since the market's inception in 2007. Make it a tradition to purchase the annual Christmas in Cowtown ornament, designed by Christopher Radko.

3401 W Lancaster Ave., 682-235-1105
www.juniorleaguefw.org

97

BUY A PAIR OF BOOTS
FROM THE JUSTIN BOOT OUTLET

The globally recognized authentic western boot company—founded in 1879—is headquartered right here in Fort Worth and has been since 1925. So, support the home brand with a trip to the factory outlet store, where there are more than 15,000 boots to choose from. Because the store is an outlet, boots range from close-outs and discontinued styles to some with small defects that are barely visible, which means there are good deals to be found. (You can feel good about splurging on those snakeskin or ostrich pair.) Don't forget a pair for the kids. Also find other brands in the Justin family like Tony Lama, Nocona, and Chippewa. The store also offers leather belts, ballcaps, cowboy hats, handbags, shirts, and casual footwear.

717 W Vickery Blvd., 817-885-8089
www.justinboots.com

SPICE UP YOUR LIFE
AT PENDERY'S WORLD OF CHILES AND SPICES

Step through the doors of this charming craftsman house to find hundreds of dried chiles and spices from regions near and far, neatly displayed room by room. Pendery's has been in business for more than 150 years; it was established when a debonair Ohio native named DeWitt Clinton Pendery arrived in Fort Worth in 1870. Back then, customers were reached by way of horse-drawn stagecoach. Today, the internet fulfills orders from around the world. The place is perfect for a unique souvenir or gift—everyone can use fajita seasoning or a custom Texas blend for chili. If you're local, consider a stop here instead of at a chain grocery store when you've run out of granulated garlic, black peppercorns, or that really hard-to-find spice for a special recipe.

1407 8th Ave., 817-924-3434
www.penderys.com

BUY FRESH EGGS
AT THE CLEARFORK FARMERS MARKET

Established in 2016, this year-round outdoor market provides for expansive views of the Trinity River as it sits right above the water's edge. Held Saturdays from 8 a.m. to noon, the market features more than two dozen local farmer, rancher, and artisan vendors—and the list keeps growing. It's a go-to for gifts, from fresh-baked pies and sourdough bread to candles and honey. While it's not the only farmers market in town, it is perhaps the most popular for its location along the Trinity Trails. Runners and cyclists arrive early for a pre- or post-workout coffee and scone, while the brunch crowd visiting nearby hot spot, Press Café (located just steps away), moseys around for impulse buys like handmade jewelry and tamales to-go.

4801 Edwards Ranch Rd.
www.farmersmarket1848.com

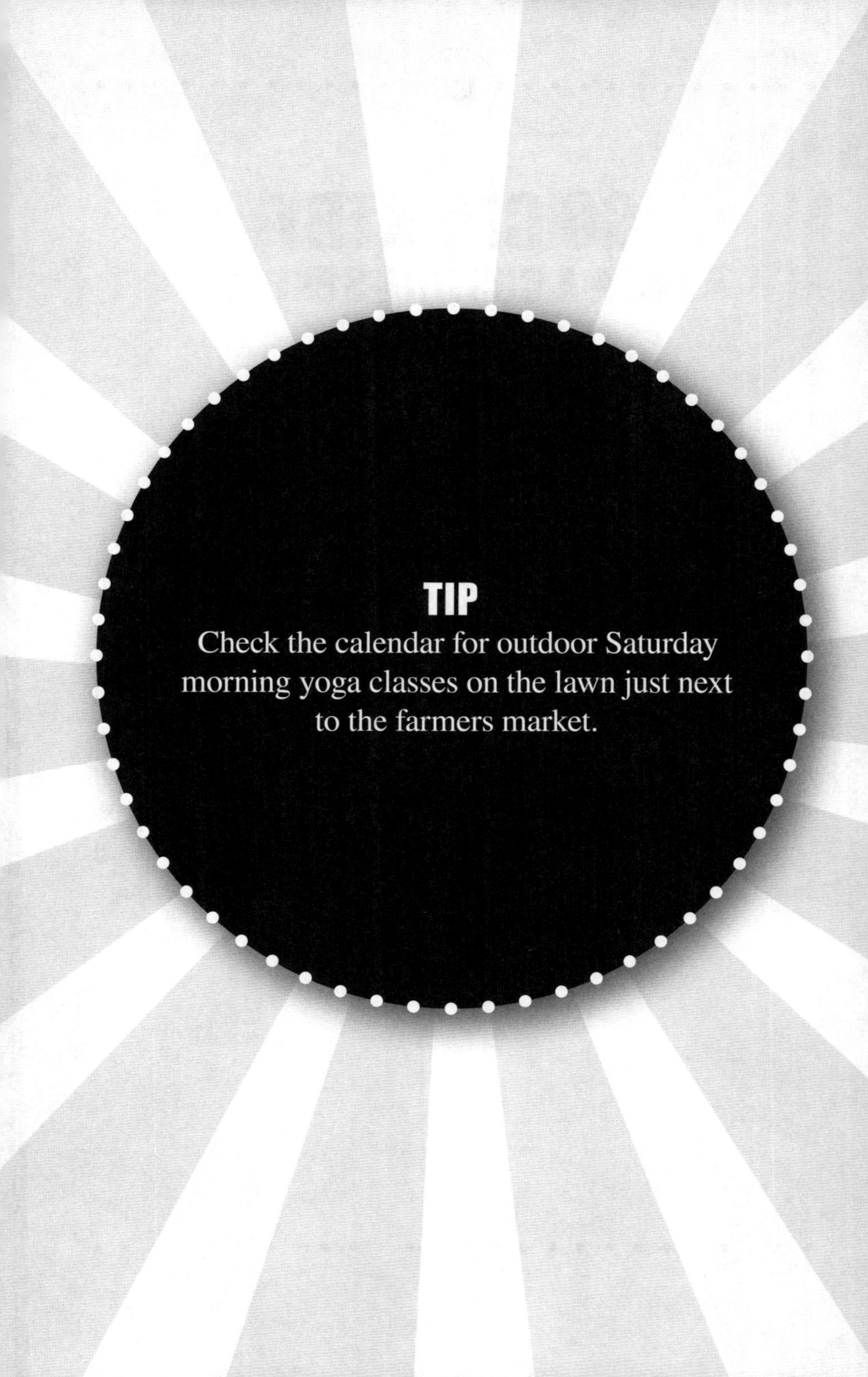
TIP
Check the calendar for outdoor Saturday morning yoga classes on the lawn just next to the farmers market.

100

GO COUNTRY
WITH A CUSTOM-SHAPED COWBOY HAT

From the crown to the brim, a cowboy hat's shape matters. No one knows this more than the professional shapers who use steam and skill to perfect hats of all kinds at the numerous hat shops in town. The Fort Worth Stockyards is no doubt the hub for cowboy-hat-buying, where tenured stores like The Best Hat Store, Sean Ryon's Western Store & Saddle Shop, Maverick Fine Western Wear, Fincher's White Front, and M. L. Leddy's have hand-creased hats for decades. Don't miss Peters Brothers Hats downtown. At least five generations of Peters have run the hat shop for more than a century, outfitting the likes of President Lyndon B. Johnson, Tom Landry, Neil Diamond, and countless celebrities. Can't decide between straw or felt? Get one of each material so you'll be prepared for both cold and warm weather.

Best Hat Store
2739 N Main St., 817-625-6650
www.besthatstore.com

Fincher's White Front
115 E Exchange Ave., 817-624-7302
www.fincherswhitefront.com

M. L. Leddy's
2455 N Main St., 817-624-3149
www.leddys.com

Maverick Fine Western Wear
100 E Exchange Ave., 817-626-1129
www.maverickwesternwear.com

Peters Brothers Hats
909 Houston St., 817-335-1715
www.pbhats.com

Sean Ryon Western Wear & Saddle Shop
2707 N Main St., 817-626-5390
www.seanryon.com

Photo credit: Caroline Daniel

ACTIVITIES
BY SEASON

WINTER

SPRING

SUMMER

FALL

SUGGESTED
ITINERARIES

OUTDOOR EXCURSIONS

DATE NIGHT

FAMILY FRIENDLY

COWBOY UP

TASTE OF FORT WORTH IN A DAY

COWTOWN'S HISTORIC AND CULTURAL GEMS

OUT ON THE TOWN

Photo credit: Japanese Palace

INDEX

Photo credit: Blissful Sky Photography